AF803162

Enterprise Fortress

Enterprise Fortress is a comprehensive guide to building secure and resilient enterprise architectures, aimed at professionals navigating the complex world of cybersecurity. Authored by cybersecurity leader Alex Stevens, the book brings together his experience of over 20 years, blending technical expertise with business strategy. It covers everything from foundational principles to advanced topics, focusing on aligning security with organisational goals. What sets this book apart is its practical, real-world focus – grounded in hands-on experience and strategic insights, it provides actionable advice that can be immediately applied.

This book equips readers with the knowledge to tackle the evolving landscape of cybersecurity. Whether you're developing security frameworks, handling governance and compliance, or leading a security team, *Enterprise Fortress* has you covered. By combining best practices with innovation, it provides tools and strategies for both current challenges and future threats.

Key Features:

- Clear, step-by-step instructions on designing and implementing enterprise security architectures.
- Practical frameworks for integrating security into the business strategy.
- Detailed insights into governance, risk management, and compliance with regulations like GDPR and ISO 27001.
- Case studies that highlight real-world challenges and solutions from various industries.
- Exploration of advanced topics like security automation, orchestration, and emerging cyber threats.
- Guidance on building and leading effective cybersecurity teams and fostering a security-aware culture within organisations.

Enterprise Fortress is perfect for cybersecurity professionals, IT leaders, enterprise architects, and business executives responsible for securing their organisations. Whether you're an experienced architect or new to the field, this book offers the technical know-how and leadership insights to help you strengthen your organisation's security posture and stay ahead of emerging threats.

Enterprise Fortress

The Ultimate Handbook for Enterprise Security Architecture

Alex Stevens

CRC Press
Taylor & Francis Group
Boca Raton London New York

CRC Press is an imprint of the
Taylor & Francis Group, an **informa** business

Designed cover image: © Shutterstock

First edition published 2025
by CRC Press
2385 NW Executive Center Drive, Suite 320, Boca Raton FL 33431

and by CRC Press
4 Park Square, Milton Park, Abingdon, Oxon, OX14 4RN
CRC Press is an imprint of Taylor & Francis Group, LLC

© 2025 Alex Stevens

Reasonable efforts have been made to publish reliable data and information, but the author and publisher cannot assume responsibility for the validity of all materials or the consequences of their use. The authors and publishers have attempted to trace the copyright holders of all material reproduced in this publication and apologize to copyright holders if permission to publish in this form has not been obtained. If any copyright material has not been acknowledged please write and let us know so we may rectify in any future reprint.

Except as permitted under U.S. Copyright Law, no part of this book may be reprinted, reproduced, transmitted, or utilized in any form by any electronic, mechanical, or other means, now known or hereafter invented, including photocopying, microfilming, and recording, or in any information storage or retrieval system, without written permission from the publishers.

For permission to photocopy or use material electronically from this work, access www.copyright.com or contact the Copyright Clearance Center, Inc. (CCC), 222 Rosewood Drive, Danvers, MA 01923, 978-750-8400. For works that are not available on CCC please contact mpkbookspermissions@tandf.co.uk

Trademark notice: Product or corporate names may be trademarks or registered trademarks and are used only for identification and explanation without intent to infringe.

ISBN: 978-1-032-95539-1 (hbk)
ISBN: 978-1-032-95645-9 (pbk)
ISBN: 978-1-003-58592-3 (ebk)

DOI: 10.1201/9781003585923

Typeset in Adobe Caslon Pro
by Deanta Global Publishing Services, Chennai, India

Contents

About the Author

Alex Stevens is a seasoned cybersecurity leader and architect with over twenty years of experience in guiding organisations to protect and optimise their digital environments. Specialising in designing security frameworks that align with business strategy, Alex has led teams and overseen the development of systems that keep businesses secure while driving operational efficiency. His leadership in cybersecurity management has been instrumental in helping organisations stay ahead of emerging threats.

Passionate about the role technology plays in business, Alex believes that effective cybersecurity is essential to enable growth. His expertise spans secure systems design, data analytics, and privacy compliance, including GDPR, as well as implementing industry standards such as ISO 27001. In leadership roles, Alex has driven innovation, managed cybersecurity strategies, and built resilient, scalable systems that prepare organisations for the future.

Alex's motivation comes from delivering peace of mind to business leaders, knowing that their technology is working *for* them, not against them. Committed to staying at the forefront of cybersecurity trends, he actively engages with industry professionals, ensuring his strategies are innovative and future-proof. Beyond managing security risks, Alex thrives on fostering a culture of cybersecurity awareness and resilience within the organisations he works with.

Acknowledgements

I would like to thank both Douglas Penn Stickly and Kristian Leeson for their support and review of this book. This book would never have been finished without their insight and encouragement.

I would also like to thank my wife Anja and my two daughters Ebony and Rosslyn for their support, love, and patience while I completed this work.

Thank you all, your unwavering support has meant the world to me!

1

Introduction to Enterprise Security Architecture

Understanding Enterprise Security Architecture

Let's kick things off by getting to grips with what Enterprise Security Architecture (ESA) actually is. Imagine ESA as the blueprint, the master plan, for safeguarding an organisation's information systems from all sorts of risks and threats. But it's not just about installing some security software and calling it a day, unfortunately it's far more intricate and complex than that. ESA is a comprehensive strategy that spans planning, designing, implementing, and managing a whole range of security policies, procedures, and technologies to protect your organisation's digital assets.

Think of ESA as the strategic framework that aims to make sure every aspect of your business is shielded from potential dangers. But here's the challenge, it's not just a set of technical tasks. ESA is about weaving security into the very fabric of your business operations. It aligns your security efforts with your broader organisational goals, creating a secure environment that's not only reactive but also resilient, always aiming to stay a step ahead of emerging threats.

Today's enterprises are up against a rapidly and constantly changing threat landscape. Cybercriminals are getting smarter, using cutting-edge technology like AI and automation to find and exploit vulnerabilities. So, ESA isn't just about defending your technical environment; it's about embedding security at every layer of your organisation. By taking a holistic approach, as represented by Figure 1.1 below, ESA ensures that every department, from IT to HR, is working together to protect your organisation's most valuable assets.

DOI: 10.1201/9781003585923-1

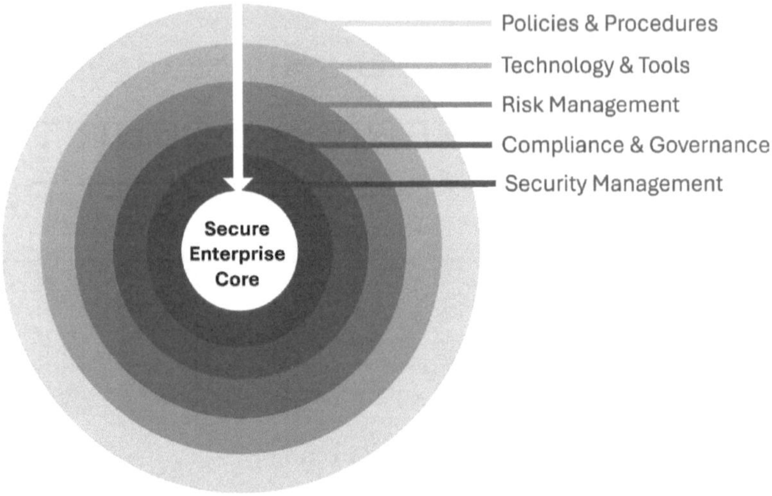

Figure 1.1 A visual layered structure of enterprise security architectural elements.

Components of Enterprise Security Architecture

Let's break down the key components that make up ESA:

- **Policies and Procedures:** These are the foundation of your security strategy. Policies set the standards for how security is managed across your organisation, making sure that everyone, from the boardroom to the mailroom, knows their role in keeping things secure. Procedures take these policies and turn them into actionable steps, creating a consistent framework that guides daily security decisions. For instance, a solid data protection policy will outline exactly how sensitive information should be handled, from collection to deletion. Procedures tied to this policy would include steps like data encryption, access controls, and secure disposal methods, ensuring that sensitive data is protected at every stage.
- **Technologies and Tools:** Think of these as the essential armour and weapons in your security arsenal. Tools like firewalls, encryption technologies, intrusion detection systems, and advanced threat intelligence platforms protect your digital infrastructure. But here's the thing, these tools aren't just for defence. They're crucial in building a proactive

security posture. For example, modern Endpoint Detection and Response (EDR) systems don't just spot threats; they analyse patterns and even predict potential attacks, keeping you a step ahead of cybercriminals.

- **Risk Management:** Effective risk management is the heart and soul of ESA. It's all about identifying potential threats, assessing their impact, and implementing measures to mitigate those risks. Risk management in ESA isn't a one-time task, it's a continuous process. For example, after a risk assessment reveals vulnerabilities in your cloud infrastructure, you might need to revise your cloud security policies, deploy additional encryption, and conduct regular audits to stay ahead of new threats.
- **Compliance and Governance:** In today's regulatory environment, compliance isn't just important, it's non-negotiable. Laws and regulations like GDPR, HIPAA, and PCI DSS impose strict requirements on how organisations handle and protect sensitive data. ESA integrates compliance into the core of your organisation, ensuring that your security measures meet all legal and regulatory requirements. Governance plays a crucial role here, providing oversight to ensure that compliance measures are implemented correctly and consistently. This involves establishing clear roles and responsibilities, conducting regular audits, and maintaining transparency with stakeholders about your organisation's security posture.
- **Security Management:** Despite the best defences, security incidents are inevitable. That's why having a defined security management approach with a robust incident response plan is critical. This component of ESA focuses on preparing for, detecting, responding to, and recovering from security incidents. Security management isn't just about minimising damage, it's about learning from past incidents to prevent future ones. For instance, a post-incident analysis might reveal gaps in your threat detection capabilities, prompting you to enhance your monitoring systems and update your incident response procedures.

Objectives of Enterprise Security Architecture

Understanding the objectives of ESA helps us appreciate why it's so important. Here's what ESA aims to achieve:

- **Alignment with Business Goals:** Security isn't just a box to tick; it's a strategic enabler of business success. ESA ensures that security measures align with your business objectives, supporting secure operations and enabling growth while protecting your assets. For example, if your organisation is expanding into new markets, ESA will guide the integration of security into this expansion, ensuring that new offices or systems are secured from day one.
- **Risk Management:** A primary goal of ESA is to manage and reduce risks to an acceptable level. This involves identifying potential threats, assessing their likelihood and impact, and implementing controls to mitigate these risks. Take, for example, a financial institution facing a growing threat of ransomware attacks. ESA would guide the implementation of enhanced backup strategies, employee training programmes, and advanced threat detection systems to keep these risks in check.
- **Compliance:** Meeting legal and regulatory requirements is crucial to avoiding penalties and protecting your organisation's reputation. ESA helps ensure that your security controls are aligned with these requirements, whether it's safeguarding customer data under GDPR or securing healthcare information in compliance with HIPAA. Beyond just ticking boxes, ESA can give your organisation a competitive edge by showing your commitment to security and data protection.
- **Resilience and Continuity:** ESA aims to ensure that your business can continue to operate smoothly, even in the face of security incidents. This is achieved through robust disaster recovery and business continuity plans that minimise downtime and ensure a quick recovery. For example, imagine a retail company with a strong ESA in place, if their primary data centre goes down, their well-rehearsed disaster recovery plan would allow them to switch to a backup facility with

minimal disruption, ensuring customers can keep shopping without interruption.

- **Cost-Effectiveness:** Implementing security measures can be costly, but ESA helps balance security needs with budget constraints. By prioritising risks and focusing on the most critical areas, ESA ensures that your security investments are cost-effective and provide maximum protection without breaking the bank.

Importance of Security Architecture in Today's Enterprises

The importance of a robust security architecture can't be overstated. Cyber threats are more advanced and pervasive than ever, from data breaches to sophisticated ransomware attacks that can cripple entire organisations. Here's why a strong ESA is vital:

- **Protecting Sensitive Data:** Sensitive information, like personal data, health records, financial details, and intellectual property, is a prime target for cybercriminals. A well-implemented ESA protects this data through encryption, strict access controls, and regular security assessments. For instance, a healthcare organisation with a comprehensive ESA can ensure that patient records are encrypted and access is strictly controlled, reducing the risk of data breaches and ensuring compliance with regulations like GDPR and HIPAA.
- **Ensuring Regulatory Compliance:** Different industries are governed by various laws and regulations that mandate specific security measures. Failing to comply with these can lead to severe penalties and damage to your organisation's reputation. ESA ensures that your organisation not only meets these requirements but also stays ahead of potential changes in the regulatory landscape. Consider the financial services sector, where regulations like PCI DSS require stringent data protection measures. An ESA aligned with these standards helps financial institutions avoid hefty fines and maintain customer trust.
- **Mitigating Risks:** Every organisation faces unique security risks based on its size, industry, and the specific threats it

encounters. ESA helps identify these risks, assess their potential impact, and implement strategies to mitigate them. For example, a global manufacturer might face risks related to industrial espionage or supply chain disruptions. ESA would guide the implementation of security measures tailored to these risks, such as enhancing network security, securing supply chains, and conducting regular risk assessments.

- **Ensuring Business Continuity:** Security incidents can cause significant disruptions, leading to operational downtime, financial losses, and damage to your brand's reputation. A well-designed ESA includes comprehensive disaster recovery and business continuity plans that enable your organisation to recover quickly from incidents with minimal disruption. Imagine a global retail chain that experiences a cyberattack on its e-commerce platform. A robust ESA would ensure that the company can quickly isolate the affected systems, restore operations from backups, and keep customer data secure, minimising the impact on business operations and customer trust.
- **Supporting Digital Transformation:** As businesses increasingly adopt new technologies like cloud computing, IoT, and AI, they also encounter new security challenges. ESA ensures that these innovations are integrated securely, allowing your organisation to embrace digital transformation without compromising security. For instance, a manufacturing company leveraging IoT devices to optimise production processes must ensure that these devices are secured against cyber threats. ESA would guide the implementation of security controls such as network segmentation, device authentication, and continuous monitoring to protect these critical operational systems.

Objectives and Scope of the Book

This book is your go-to guide for understanding and implementing Enterprise Security Architecture. We've taken complex security concepts and broken them down into accessible, practical advice that's tailored to a broad audience. Whether you're a seasoned security professional, an IT architect, or someone simply interested in cybersecurity, this book is designed to equip you with the knowledge and tools needed to build and manage secure enterprise environments.

Key Topics Covered

- **Foundations of Enterprise Security:** We'll start with the basics, covering key concepts, security principles, and regulatory requirements to establish a strong foundation for your security architecture.
- **Enterprise Security Architecture Frameworks:** Next, we'll explore popular frameworks like TOGAF, SABSA, and the NIST Cybersecurity Framework, discussing how to apply them effectively in your organisation.
- **Security Governance and Risk Management:** We'll delve into how to establish governance structures, develop risk management processes, and create security policies, standards, and procedures that align with your organisation's goals.
- **Building Blocks of Security Architecture:** This section covers essential components like Identity and Access Management (IAM), network security, application security, data security, and cloud security, providing a comprehensive view of how to protect your organisation's assets.
- **Designing Security Architectures:** You'll learn the principles of security architecture design, including how to integrate security into different environments and how to scale your architecture as your organisation grows.
- **Implementing Security Solutions:** We'll share best practices for selecting, implementing, and managing security technologies, with a focus on achieving a balance between security and operational efficiency.
- **Advanced Topics in Enterprise Security:** From emerging threats and the role of AI in security to Zero Trust architecture and security in DevOps, we'll cover the cutting-edge topics that are shaping the future of enterprise security.
- **Subject-Specific Topics in Enterprise Security:** In the later chapters, we'll dive into specialised areas such as Governance, Risk, and Compliance (GRC); Security Operations Centres

(SOC); Incident Response and Management; Security Automation and Orchestration; Building a Security-Aware Culture; Preparing for Cybersecurity Careers; Emerging Threats and Future Trends; and Developing and Implementing a Cybersecurity Strategy. These chapters provide in-depth coverage of critical aspects of enterprise security that are essential for addressing the unique challenges of modern organisations.

- **Evaluating and Improving Security Posture:** We'll guide you on how to assess and improve your security set-up, using metrics and Key Performance Indicators (KPIs) to measure effectiveness and drive continuous improvement.
- **Enhancing and Maturing Security Operations:** This section will discuss strategies for integrating security with IT operations, automating security tasks, and fostering a collaborative SecOps culture to ensure long-term security success.
- **Future Trends and Developments:** We'll look ahead to the future of cybersecurity, discussing how to prepare for upcoming challenges and stay ahead of the curve in a rapidly changing threat landscape.
- **Case Studies and Real-World Examples:** Throughout the book, we'll share success stories, lessons from security breaches, and practical applications of security architecture principles to help you apply what you've learned in real-world scenarios.

Who Should Read This Book?

This book is intended for a wide range of readers, including:

- **Security Professionals:** If you're responsible for managing or implementing security measures in an organisation, this book will serve as a valuable resource, offering insights and strategies to enhance your security architecture.
- **IT Architects and Engineers:** For those involved in designing and maintaining IT infrastructure, this book provides essential guidance on integrating security into your architectural

designs and ensuring that security is a core component of your IT operations.

- **Business Leaders:** Executives and managers who want to understand how security contributes to achieving business objectives will find this book enlightening. It will help you make informed decisions about security investments and align security initiatives with your business goals.
- **Students and Academics:** If you're studying cybersecurity or related fields, this book offers a comprehensive overview of enterprise security architecture, providing a solid foundation for your studies and future career.
- **Anyone Interested in Cybersecurity:** Whether you're new to the field or looking to deepen your knowledge, this book is packed with useful information and practical advice that will help you navigate the complex world of enterprise security.

By the end of this book, you'll have a deep understanding of how to develop and maintain a secure enterprise architecture that can withstand the ever-changing cyber threat landscape. You'll be equipped with the knowledge and tools to protect your organisation's assets, ensure compliance, and support business growth in a secure and resilient manner.

Case in Point

Let's consider a large financial institution that handles sensitive customer data. Without a strong security architecture, it could be vulnerable to data breaches, leading to financial losses, legal penalties, and damage to its reputation. By implementing a comprehensive security architecture, this institution can safeguard its assets, ensure compliance with regulations, and maintain its service integrity and customer trust.

For example, one real-world case involves a financial services company that was repeatedly targeted by cyberattacks. Lacking a cohesive security strategy, they suffered multiple breaches. After a significant data breach exposed customer information, they decided to overhaul their security architecture using the SABSA framework. This helped them align their security measures with business goals, implement robust Identity and Access Management (IAM) solutions, enhance network security, and set up continuous monitoring. The result? They drastically reduced the risk of future breaches, protected customer data, and restored their market reputation.

Another example is a healthcare organisation that fell victim to a ransomware attack, crippling its operations. Their lack of preparation and weak security measures made them an easy target. After the attack, they adopted a comprehensive ESA that included advanced threat detection, regular security assessments, and staff training programmes. This not only improved their security posture but also ensured better compliance with healthcare regulations and boosted patient trust.

And finally, consider a global retail chain that experienced a major security incident due to a vulnerability in its e-commerce platform. The breach led to the exposure of customer payment information and a subsequent loss of trust and revenue. By implementing a comprehensive ESA, the company was able to strengthen its security posture, enhance its incident response capabilities, and rebuild customer trust through transparency and improved security measures. The ESA guided the implementation of a multi-layered security approach, including robust encryption, strict access controls, and continuous monitoring, which collectively ensured the long-term security of the company's assets.

Final Thoughts

As we journey through this book, we'll explore various aspects of Enterprise Security Architecture, offering practical insights and actionable strategies that you can apply in your organisation. Whether you're new to security or looking to deepen your knowledge, this book is designed to be your ultimate guide to building a secure, resilient enterprise.

Next up, we'll dive into the foundational concepts and terminologies in enterprise security architecture and cybersecurity, laying the groundwork for a deeper exploration of Enterprise Security Architecture. Let's get started!

2
Foundations of Enterprise Security

Basic Concepts and Terminologies

Before we go deeper into the world of enterprise security, let's start with the basics. Understanding the foundational concepts of cybersecurity and its key terminologies is crucial because these are the building blocks for everything we'll discuss in later chapters. So, let's break these down in simple, digestible terms.

Core Pillars of Cybersecurity: The CIA Triad

When we talk about cybersecurity, there's one fundamental concept that forms the bedrock of everything: the Confidentiality, Integrity, Availability (CIA) Triad (Figure 2.1). And no, it's not some secret agency! The CIA Triad is a straightforward yet powerful model that helps us protect information in the digital world.

- **Confidentiality:** This is all about keeping information under lock and key, ensuring that only those who are supposed to access it can do so. Think of it like locking your diary with a key that only you possess. In the digital realm, we achieve confidentiality through methods like encryption and access control.
- **Integrity:** Integrity ensures that information remains unaltered unless it's supposed to be changed. Imagine a tamper-proof seal on a product; if the seal is broken, you know something's been messed with. In IT, integrity is maintained using tools like checksums, hashing, and digital signatures.

DOI: 10.1201/9781003585923-2

Figure 2.1 The CIA triad: confidentiality, integrity, and availability—the three essential pillars of cybersecurity.

- **Availability:** Availability is about making sure that information and resources are accessible when authorised users need them. It's like keeping a shop open during business hours, customers should be able to access products when they want. We protect availability with security controls like Denial of Service (DoS) protection and redundant systems.

Key Terms and Definitions

To navigate the landscape of enterprise security, you need to be familiar with a few key terms. Let's define these in straightforward language:

- **Threat:** A threat is anything that could potentially cause harm to an information system. This could range from a hacker trying to breach your network to an employee accidentally deleting important files. Threats can come from inside or outside your organisation and can be intentional or accidental.
- **Vulnerability:** Think of vulnerabilities as chinks in your armour, weak spots that a threat can exploit. These could be due to software bugs, misconfigurations, or even a lack of security controls.

- **Risk:** Risk is the potential for loss or damage when a threat exploits a vulnerability. It's calculated by considering both the likelihood of the event and its impact. For instance, the risk of a data breach involves assessing how likely it is to happen and how much damage it could cause.
- **Attack Vector:** This is the path or method an attacker uses to access your system. Common attack vectors include phishing emails, malware, or exploiting software vulnerabilities.
- **Mitigation:** Mitigation refers to the steps you take to reduce the risk or impact of a security incident. This can include technical controls like firewalls and antivirus software or organisational policies and procedures.
- **Authentication:** Authentication is the process of proving that someone is who they say they are. Common methods include passwords, biometrics (like fingerprints), and multi-factor authentication (MFA), which require multiple forms of verification before access is granted.
- **Authorisation:** Once someone is authenticated, authorisation determines what they can access. It's like checking someone's ticket at a concert to see if they have access to VIP areas. Authorisation is often managed through Access Control Lists (ACLs) or Role-Based Access Control (RBAC).
- **Encryption:** Encryption is the process of converting data into a code to prevent unauthorised access. Encryption can be applied to data at rest (like files on a disk), in transit (like emails), or in use (like data being processed).
- **Firewall:** Think of a firewall as the bouncer at a club. It monitors and controls incoming and outgoing network traffic based on security rules. Firewalls can be configured to block unwanted traffic and allow only legitimate connections.
- **Intrusion Detection System (IDS):** IDS is like a security camera that watches for suspicious activity on your network or systems. It doesn't stop the activity but raises the alarm when something fishy is detected, allowing security teams to respond quickly.
- **Intrusion Prevention System (IPS):** Similar to IDS, but an IPS takes things a step further by actively blocking detected

threats. It's like having a security guard who not only detects intruders but also stops them in their tracks.

- **Security Information and Event Management (SIEM):** SIEM is the command centre of your security operations. It collects and analyses security alerts generated by network hardware and applications, giving you a real-time view of what's happening across your systems.
- **Patch Management:** Patch management is the process of keeping software up to date by regularly applying patches or updates to fix vulnerabilities. Effective patch management is crucial for maintaining the security of systems and applications.

Security Principles

There are several fundamental principles that guide how we design and implement security measures. These principles ensure that our security efforts are effective and aligned with our organisation's goals.

- **Least Privilege:** Only give users and systems the access they absolutely need to do their jobs, no more, no less. This limits the damage that can be done if an account is compromised. For example, an employee in finance doesn't need access to HR records, and applying the principle of least privilege ensures they can't access this data.
- **Defence in Depth:** Don't rely on just one layer of security. If one control fails, others are there to back it up. It's like wearing a seatbelt, having airbags, and driving a car with crash protection, multiple layers of safety.
- **Separation of Duties:** Split up critical tasks among different people to reduce the risk of mistakes or fraud. It's like having one person handle the money and another person do the accounting. This principle is especially important in financial systems to prevent fraud and errors.
- **Fail-Safe Defaults:** If something goes wrong, the system should default to a secure state. For example, if a security mechanism fails, it should lock things down rather than

leaving everything open. This principle helps prevent unauthorised access during system failures.

- **Security by Design:** Build security into the system from the ground up, rather than trying to bolt it on afterward. It's like designing a house with security features in mind, rather than trying to add them later. This approach ensures that security is integrated into every stage of the system's development.
- **Minimise Attack Surface:** Reduce the number of ways an attacker can get into your system by eliminating unnecessary services, protocols, and applications. The smaller the attack surface, the fewer opportunities there are for attackers to exploit vulnerabilities.
- **Layered Security:** Similar to Defence in Depth, this involves using multiple layers of security controls to make it harder for attackers to succeed. For instance, you might combine firewalls, IDS/IPS, encryption, and access controls to protect your network.
- **User Training and Awareness:** Make sure users understand security policies and best practices so they can help prevent things like social engineering attacks. Educating users about the risks and how to respond to them is a key component of an effective security strategy.
- **Regular Audits and Assessments:** Keep checking for vulnerabilities and compliance with security policies through regular audits and assessments. This ongoing process helps identify and address security gaps before they can be exploited by attackers.

Regulatory and Compliance Requirements

Every organisation must adhere to various laws and regulations designed to protect sensitive information. Let's go over some of the key regulations you are likely to encounter:

- **General Data Protection Regulation (GDPR):** GDPR is all about protecting personal data for individuals within the European Union and the UK. It gives people rights over their data, like the right to access, correct, or delete it. It also requires organisations to notify authorities if there's a data breach. Non-compliance can lead to hefty fines, so meeting GDPR requirements is crucial.

- **Health Insurance Portability and Accountability Act (HIPAA):** This US regulation protects sensitive patient information. It sets standards for the security and privacy of medical records, requiring healthcare providers to secure electronic protected health information (ePHI) and notify individuals in case of a breach. Failing to comply with HIPAA can result in significant penalties and damage to an organisation's reputation.
- **Sarbanes-Oxley Act (SOX):** SOX is aimed at protecting investors by ensuring the accuracy of financial reporting. It requires senior corporate officers to certify financial statements and mandates strong internal controls. Compliance with SOX is particularly important for publicly traded companies.
- **Payment Card Industry Data Security Standard (PCI DSS):** This standard applies to any organisation that handles payment card data. It includes requirements like maintaining a secure network, protecting cardholder data, and regularly monitoring networks. Non-compliance with PCI DSS can result in fines, increased transaction fees, and even the loss of the ability to process credit card payments.
- **Federal Information Security Management Act (FISMA):** FISMA is a US federal law that requires government agencies to develop and implement security programs to protect their information systems. Compliance with FISMA ensures that federal information and systems are adequately protected against threats.
- **Network and Information Systems Directive (NIS):** The NIS Directive applies to organisations providing essential services within the EU. It aims to improve the security of network and information systems by requiring risk management and incident reporting. Compliance with the NIS Directive is crucial for organisations in sectors like energy, transportation, and finance.
- **California Consumer Privacy Act (CCPA):** The CCPA enhances privacy rights for California residents, giving them

the right to know what personal data is being collected and the right to opt out of its sale. Organisations that fail to comply with the CCPA can face significant fines and legal action.

- **ISO/IEC 27701 (Privacy Information Management System – PIMS):** This is an extension to ISO/IEC 27001 and 27002, focusing on privacy information management. It helps organisations manage personal data in compliance with regulations like GDPR. Implementing ISO/IEC 27701 can enhance an organisation's data protection efforts and demonstrate commitment to privacy.
- **System and Organisation Controls 2 (SOC 2):** SOC 2 is an auditing procedure that ensures service providers securely manage data to protect their clients' privacy. It covers areas like security, availability, processing integrity, confidentiality, and privacy. Achieving SOC 2 compliance can boost customer trust and demonstrate a commitment to security.
- **NIST SP 800-53:** This provides a catalogue of security and privacy controls for federal information systems and organisations to protect their operations and assets. Adopting NIST SP 800-53 controls can strengthen an organisation's security posture and ensure compliance with federal standards.

Security Models

To better understand how organisations manage their security, it's crucial to explore some key security models that lay the groundwork for structured security practices. Each of these models originates from different environments and focuses on specific aspects of security, making them vital tools in various industries.

- **Bell-LaPadula Model:** This model comes from military and government settings, where confidentiality is paramount. It's designed to enforce strict access control and is based on two main principles:
    - **Simple Security Property:** This rule ensures that users can't access data classified above their security clearance (no read-up).

    - **Star Property:** This principle prevents users from sharing or downgrading data by writing it to a lower security level than their own (no write-down).
- **Biba Model:** While the Bell-LaPadula model emphasises confidentiality, the Biba model focuses on maintaining data integrity, making it essential in environments where data accuracy is crucial. It's governed by two core rules:
    - **Simple Integrity Property:** This rule prevents users from compromising data integrity by restricting them from reading information from a lower integrity level (no read-down).
    - **Star Integrity Property:** This principle stops users from altering data at a higher integrity level than their own, ensuring that data remains reliable (no write-up).
- **Clark-Wilson Model:** Used predominantly in commercial environments, this model focuses on maintaining the integrity of data through controlled processes. It's particularly effective in reducing the risks of fraud and errors. The model highlights:
    - **Well-Formed Transactions:** This principle ensures that all data manipulations are performed through predefined and secure procedures.
    - **Separation of Duties:** By dividing responsibilities among different individuals, this rule mitigates the risk of unauthorised actions, promoting a more secure environment.

Understanding these models is essential because they provide the frameworks many organisations rely on to safeguard their data and operations, each tailored to specific security needs.

Building a Strong Security Culture

At the end of the day, even the best security measures won't be effective without a strong security culture. Everyone in the organisation needs to understand their role in protecting assets and take security seriously. In Chapter 15, we'll delve deeper into how to build a strong security culture within your organisation, but for now, let's cover the basics.

Elements of a Strong Security Culture

- **Leadership Commitment:** Security starts at the top. Senior management needs to lead by example, allocate resources, and set policies that demonstrate a commitment to security. When leaders prioritise security, it reinforces its importance throughout the organisation.
- **Employee Training and Awareness:** Regular training helps employees understand the importance of security and how to recognise and respond to threats. This can include phishing simulations, secure password practices, and incident reporting protocols. A well-informed workforce is a critical line of defence against cyber threats.
- **Clear Policies and Procedures:** Well-documented policies provide guidance on security practices and set expectations for everyone. These policies should be easily accessible and regularly updated to reflect new threats and changes in the regulatory landscape.
- **Incident Reporting and Response:** Encourage employees to report any security incidents and ensure there's a clear plan for responding to them. A prompt and effective response can minimise the impact of a security breach and help prevent future incidents.
- **Continuous Improvement:** Regularly review and update security practices to keep up with new threats and ensure the security program stays effective. This includes conducting regular audits, analysing incident reports, and staying informed about the latest developments in cybersecurity.

Creating a Security-Aware Workforce

Building a security-aware workforce isn't just about handing out a manual and hoping for the best. It's about ongoing education and fostering a culture where security is everyone's responsibility. Training should cover things like:

- **Phishing Awareness:** Teaching employees how to spot phishing emails and avoid falling for scams. This can be reinforced with regular phishing simulations to test and improve employee awareness.
- **Password Security:** Emphasising the importance of strong, unique passwords and not reusing them across different sites. Encourage the use of password managers to help employees manage their passwords securely.
- **Data Handling:** Educating employees on how to handle sensitive data, including encryption and secure disposal. Proper data handling practices are essential for protecting against data breaches and complying with regulations like GDPR.
- **Incident Response:** Ensuring everyone knows how to report a security incident and what steps to take. A well-prepared workforce can act quickly and effectively to minimise the impact of security incidents.

Encouraging a Proactive Security Mindset

A proactive security mindset means empowering employees to take ownership of security. Here's how you can encourage that:

- **Recognition and Rewards:** Acknowledge and reward employees who demonstrate good security practices to encourage others to follow suit. This can be done through formal recognition programmes or simple gestures of appreciation.
- **Open Communication:** Make it easy for employees to voice security concerns or suggest improvements without fear of repercussions. An open dialogue about security can help identify potential risks and foster a culture of continuous improvement.
- **Security Champions:** Designate security champions in different departments to promote awareness and best practices across the organisation. These champions can act as liaisons between the security team and the rest of the organisation, helping to reinforce the importance of security.

Case Study: Building a Security Culture in a Financial Institution

Overview

A large financial institution was grappling with a growing wave of cyber threats. While they had technical defences in place, the leadership soon realised that tech alone wasn't enough. They needed to cultivate a robust security culture across the entire organisation to stay ahead of the game.

Challenges

- **Lack of Security Culture:** Despite having technical measures in place, the institution struggled with a lack of security awareness among its employees. Many didn't fully understand the importance of their role in maintaining security, leading to vulnerabilities.
- **Employee Resistance:** There was noticeable resistance among employees towards adopting security practices. Many viewed them as a burden, making it difficult to enforce security protocols effectively.
- **Inconsistent Incident Reporting:** The institution faced issues with under-reporting of incidents. Employees were either unaware of what constituted a reportable incident or felt that reporting was too cumbersome, leading to delayed responses to potential threats.
- **Evolving Cyber Threats:** The threat landscape was continuously evolving, but the institution's security policies and training programmes weren't keeping pace. This left them vulnerable to newer forms of attacks, such as sophisticated phishing schemes.

Solutions Implemented

1. **Leadership Commitment:** The CEO and senior management took the lead in embedding security into the company's culture. They ensured that resources were allocated, and security became a key element of all business strategies.

2. **Comprehensive Training and Awareness Programmes:** Regular training sessions were conducted, focusing on real-life scenarios like phishing simulations. These programmes were designed to be engaging and practical, ensuring employees knew how to recognise and report threats.
3. **Development of Clear, Accessible Policies:** The institution crafted clear and concise security policies that were communicated across all levels of the organisation. These policies were not just rules but included practical guidance on maintaining security.
4. **Streamlined Incident Reporting Mechanism:** A new process was introduced to make it easier for employees to report suspicious activity. This mechanism was straightforward and encouraged prompt reporting, ensuring the security team could act quickly.
5. **Ongoing Review and Improvement:** The institution's security team didn't just sit on their hands. They kept practices up to date by regularly reviewing security measures and incorporating feedback from employees.

Outcomes

- **Reduced Phishing Success Rate:** All that training paid off. Employees got sharper at spotting phishing messages, and the success rate of phishing attacks dropped dramatically.
- **Increased Incident Reporting:** With a more vigilant workforce, incident reports went up. This allowed the security team to respond quicker and more effectively, cutting down the impact of potential breaches.
- **Improved Security Posture:** Overall, the institution's security game was stronger than ever. Fewer successful attacks and quicker recoveries meant the organisation was well on its way to staying ahead of evolving threats.

Conclusion

Understanding the basic concepts and terminologies in enterprise security is essential for building a robust security architecture. By familiarising yourself with these key terms, security principles, regulatory requirements, and security models, you'll be well-equipped to develop and manage a secure enterprise environment.

In the next chapter, we'll explore various enterprise security architecture frameworks. We'll dive into their components, applications, and benefits, and we'll also compare them to help you choose the one that best fits your organisation's needs and goals.

3

Enterprise Security Architecture Frameworks

Introduction to Security Frameworks

When it comes to implementing enterprise security, frameworks are like your guiding star. They provide structured, repeatable approaches for designing, implementing, and managing security within your organisation. By following a framework, you ensure that your security efforts are consistent, comprehensive, and aligned with industry best practices.

However, with so many frameworks available, each offering its unique approach, it can be challenging to choose the right one for your organisation. This chapter will help you navigate the landscape of enterprise security architecture frameworks by exploring those that are the most widely used ones. We'll discuss their strengths, weaknesses, and how they can be applied in different organisational contexts.

The Role of Frameworks in Security Architecture

Before diving into specific frameworks, it's important to understand the role they play in enterprise security architecture and the benefits they offer. A good framework provides:

- **Consistency:** Frameworks offer a consistent approach to security that can be applied across different departments, projects, and technologies. This consistency helps ensure that security measures are effective and aligned with organisational goals.
- **Scalability:** Whether you're a small business or a large multinational, frameworks are designed to be scalable. They can be

DOI: 10.1201/9781003585923-3

adapted to fit the size, complexity, and specific needs of your organisation.

- **Compliance:** Many frameworks are aligned with regulatory requirements, helping organisations meet compliance obligations and avoid penalties.
- **Risk Management:** Frameworks typically include processes for identifying, assessing, and mitigating risks. This helps organisations proactively manage security threats and reduce their potential impact.
- **Communication:** Frameworks provide a common language for discussing security within and outside the organisation. This can improve communication between technical and non-technical stakeholders, helping everyone understand the importance of security.

The Open Group Architecture Framework (TOGAF)

TOGAF is a popular framework for enterprise architecture that places a strong focus on aligning IT with business goals. While it's not exclusively a security framework, TOGAF includes comprehensive guidance on integrating security into enterprise architecture. It's particularly well-suited for large organisations looking to ensure that their security efforts are aligned with their overall business strategy.

Key Components

- **Architecture Development Method (ADM):** The core of TOGAF, ADM is a step-by-step process for developing enterprise architecture. It includes phases for defining the architecture vision, business architecture, information systems architecture, and technology architecture.
- **Security Architecture:** TOGAF treats security as a cross-cutting concern, meaning security considerations should be integrated into every phase of the ADM. This ensures that security isn't an afterthought but an integral part of the architecture.

- **Business-IT Alignment:** TOGAF emphasises the importance of aligning IT with business objectives, viewing security as an enabler of business goals.

Strengths

- **Comprehensive:** TOGAF covers all aspects of enterprise architecture, including security, making it a holistic approach.
- **Flexibility:** The ADM can be adapted to fit the specific needs of an organisation, allowing for customisation.
- **Business Focus:** TOGAF's emphasis on aligning IT with business goals ensures that security measures support the organisation's strategic objectives.

Weaknesses

- **Complexity:** TOGAF can be complex and challenging to implement, especially for smaller organisations without dedicated architecture teams.
- **Not Security-Focused:** While TOGAF includes security, it's not a security-specific framework, so organisations may need to supplement it with additional security guidelines.

Application: TOGAF is ideal for large organisations with mature IT and security teams. It's particularly useful for organisations looking to align their security efforts with their overall business strategy. For smaller organisations, TOGAF might be overkill, and a more security-focused framework could be a better fit.

Sherwood Applied Business Security Architecture (SABSA)

SABSA is a security-focused enterprise architecture framework designed to align security with business requirements. It's a risk-driven approach that integrates security into every layer of the enterprise architecture. SABSA is particularly well-suited for organisations that need a robust security architecture aligned with business goals.

Key Components

- **SABSA Matrix:** The core of the SABSA framework, this matrix comprises six layers: Contextual, Conceptual, Logical, Physical, Component, and Operational. Each layer addresses different aspects of security architecture, all aligned with business drivers to ensure that security measures support business objectives.
- **Business Attribute Profiling:** SABSA uses business attribute profiling to identify the specific security requirements of the organisation, defining security attributes like confidentiality, integrity, and availability and aligning them with business goals.
- **Risk Management:** SABSA emphasises risk management, with processes for identifying, assessing, and mitigating risks at every layer of the architecture.

Strengths

- **Business Alignment:** SABSA's focus on aligning security with business goals ensures that security measures are directly linked to business needs.
- **Risk-Driven:** SABSA's approach tailors security measures to the specific risks faced by the organisation.
- **Comprehensive:** The SABSA Matrix provides a thorough view of security architecture, covering everything from high-level strategy to detailed implementation.

Weaknesses

- **Complexity:** Like TOGAF, SABSA can be complex to implement, particularly for smaller organisations or those without dedicated security architecture teams.
- **Specialisation:** SABSA's highly specialised nature can make it difficult to integrate with other enterprise architecture frameworks.

Application: SABSA is ideal for organisations that need a strong focus on security and risk management. It's particularly useful in industries with high security requirements, such as finance, healthcare, and government. SABSA's alignment of security with business goals makes it a good choice for organisations needing to demonstrate a clear link between security and business outcomes.

NIST Cybersecurity Framework

Developed by the National Institute of Standards and Technology (NIST), the NIST Cybersecurity Framework offers a comprehensive, policy-neutral approach to managing cybersecurity risks. It's widely used across industries, particularly in the United States, where it's been adopted by both private and public sector organisations.

Key Components

- **Core:** The Core is a set of cybersecurity activities, outcomes, and informative references that are common across critical infrastructure sectors. It's divided into five functions: Identify, Protect, Detect, Respond, and Recover, providing a comprehensive view of cybersecurity risk management.
- **Implementation Tiers:** The framework includes four tiers (Partial, Risk Informed, Repeatable, and Adaptive) that describe the degree to which an organisation's cybersecurity practices are informed by risk management and the extent to which those practices are integrated into overall business practices.
- **Profiles:** Profiles help organisations align their cybersecurity activities with their business requirements, risk tolerance, and resources, representing the alignment of an organisation's cybersecurity activities with the desired outcomes of the Core.

Strengths

- **Flexibility:** The NIST framework is highly adaptable and can fit the needs of any organisation, regardless of size or industry.
- **Comprehensive:** The five functions of the Core offer a holistic approach to managing cybersecurity risks, from identification to recovery.

- **Widely Recognised:** NIST is a trusted name in cybersecurity, and its framework is widely respected across industries.

Weaknesses

- **Breadth:** The framework's broad scope can make it challenging for organisations to focus on specific areas without additional guidance.
- **Implementation:** While the framework provides a solid foundation, organisations may need additional resources or expertise to implement it effectively.

Application: The NIST Cybersecurity Framework is suitable for organisations of all sizes and across all industries. Its flexibility and comprehensive approach make it particularly useful for organisations looking to establish or improve their cybersecurity practices. It's also a good choice for organisations needing to comply with regulatory requirements, as the framework aligns with many international standards.

ISO/IEC 27001

ISO/IEC 27001 is an international standard for information security management systems (ISMS). It provides a systematic approach to managing sensitive company information, ensuring it remains secure. ISO/IEC 27001 is widely used across industries, particularly in Europe.

Key Components

- **ISMS Framework:** The ISMS framework offers a systematic approach to managing information security, covering everything from risk assessment and treatment to incident management and compliance.
- **Annex A Controls:** The standard includes a comprehensive set of controls (Annex A) that can be implemented to address specific security risks, organised into 14 categories covering everything from information security policies to supplier relationships.

- **Continuous Improvement:** ISO/IEC 27001 emphasises continuous improvement, requiring organisations to regularly review and update their security practices to keep up with evolving threats.

Strengths

- **International Recognition:** ISO/IEC 27001 is recognised worldwide, making it a valuable certification for organisations operating internationally.
- **Comprehensive:** The standard covers all aspects of information security management, providing a solid foundation for building a secure organisation.
- **Compliance:** ISO/IEC 27001 helps organisations meet regulatory requirements, aligning with many international standards.

Weaknesses

- **Certification Process:** Achieving ISO/IEC 27001 certification can be a lengthy and resource-intensive process, particularly for smaller organisations.
- **Complexity:** The standard's comprehensive nature can make it difficult to implement without dedicated resources or expertise.

Application: ISO/IEC 27001 is ideal for organisations looking to establish a formal, structured approach to information security management. It's particularly useful for organisations operating in regulated industries or those needing to demonstrate compliance with international standards. The standard's emphasis on continuous improvement also makes it a good choice for organisations committed to maintaining a high level of security over time.

Control Objectives for Information and Related Technologies (COBIT)

COBIT is a framework for the governance and management of enterprise IT. Developed by ISACA, COBIT offers a comprehensive framework for managing IT processes and aligning them with business goals. While not exclusively a security framework, COBIT provides extensive guidance on integrating security into IT governance.

Key Components

- **Governance and Management Objectives:** COBIT defines governance and management objectives covering all aspects of IT, including security, helping organisations ensure IT supports business goals and meets regulatory requirements.
- **Process Model:** COBIT includes a detailed process model that provides guidance on implementing governance and management objectives, covering everything from planning and organisation to delivery and support.
- **Capability Levels:** COBIT defines capability levels for each process, allowing organisations to assess their current maturity and set targets for improvement.

Strengths

- **Alignment with Business Goals:** COBIT's focus on aligning IT with business objectives ensures that security measures support organisational goals.
- **Comprehensive:** The framework covers all aspects of IT governance, offering a holistic approach to managing IT and security.
- **Maturity Assessment:** COBIT's capability levels allow organisations to assess their current maturity and set targets for improvement.

Weaknesses

- **Complexity:** COBIT can be complex to implement, particularly for smaller organisations or those without dedicated IT governance teams.
- **Not Security-Focused:** While COBIT includes security, it's not a security-specific framework, so organisations may need to supplement it with additional security guidelines.

Application: COBIT is ideal for organisations looking to align their IT governance with business goals. It's particularly useful for large organisations with mature IT processes that need to integrate security into their IT governance framework. For smaller organisations or those focused exclusively on security, a more security-specific framework might be a better fit.

Comparison of Frameworks

Each of these frameworks offers unique strengths and is suited to different organisational needs. Here's a quick comparison to help you decide which framework might be the best fit for your organisations needs (Table 3.1):

- **TOGAF:** Best for large organisations looking to align IT and security with business strategy. It's comprehensive but may be complex for smaller organisations.
- **SABSA:** Ideal for organisations needing a strong focus on security and risk management. It's highly specialised and aligns security with business goals.
- **NIST Cybersecurity Framework:** Suitable for organisations of all sizes and industries, offering flexibility and a comprehensive approach to cybersecurity.
- **ISO/IEC 27001:** Best for organisations looking for a formal, structured approach to information security management, particularly those in regulated industries.
- **COBIT:** Ideal for organisations looking to integrate security into IT governance and align IT with business goals. It's comprehensive but may be complex to implement.

Case Study: Choosing the Right Framework

A mid-sized financial services company found itself at a crossroads. They needed to boost their security posture while also staying compliant with industry regulations. With the pressure on, the leadership team started exploring different frameworks to find the best fit for their needs.

TABLE 3.1 Comparison of Security Architectural Frameworks

FRAMEWORK	FEATURES	BEST USE CASE	STRENGTHS	WEAKNESSES
TOGAF	Comprehensive enterprise architecture	Enterprise-wide architecture	Aligns IT with business goals	Complexity
SABSA	Security-focused enterprise architecture	Security and risk management	Aligns security with business needs	Specialised and complex
NIST	Cybersecurity risk management	Cybersecurity across industries	Flexible and comprehensive	Broad, can be too general
ISO 27001	Information security management	Compliance and ISMS	Globally recognised	Lengthy certification process
COBIT	IT governance	IT and security governance	Aligns IT with business goals	Complexity

Challenges

- **Regulatory Pressure:** Operating in a highly regulated environment, the company faced constant pressure to meet stringent data protection and risk management requirements.
- **Security and IT Governance Integration:** The company wanted to not only tighten security but also integrate it into their broader IT governance efforts.
- **Choosing the Right Framework:** With several options on the table, each with its strengths and complexities, the company had to determine which framework, or combination of frameworks, would best serve their needs without overwhelming their resources.

Options Considered

1. **TOGAF:** Comprehensive but complex, TOGAF was considered for its enterprise-wide architecture capabilities. However, its focus on broader IT architecture made it less appealing for the company's specific security focus.
2. **SABSA:** Known for aligning security with business goals and focusing on risk management, SABSA's approach to business attribute profiling was particularly appealing for managing the company's specific risks.
3. **NIST Cybersecurity Framework:** The flexibility and broad scope of the NIST framework made it an attractive option, especially for covering cybersecurity risks across the organisation.
4. **ISO/IEC 27001:** Given the company's need for a structured, formal approach to managing information security, ISO/IEC 27001 was a strong candidate. It also aligned with the company's regulatory requirements.
5. **COBIT:** The company's interest in integrating security with IT governance made COBIT a contender, though its complexity was a concern.

Decision

After weighing the pros and cons, the company opted for a hybrid approach. They chose *SABSA* to lead their security architecture and risk management efforts, aligning perfectly with their business-driven focus. To formalise their information security management system, they implemented *ISO/IEC 27001*, which provided the structure and compliance they needed. Finally, they incorporated elements of the *NIST Cybersecurity Framework* to ensure they covered all their cybersecurity bases. This blend allowed them to meet their security goals, stay compliant, and align their efforts with business objectives.

Conclusion

Choosing the right enterprise security architecture framework is a critical decision that will shape your organisation's security posture for years to come. Each framework offers unique strengths, and the best choice will depend on your organisation's size, industry, and specific security needs. By understanding the key components and applications of each framework, you'll be better equipped to select the one that aligns with your business goals and supports your security objectives.

In the next chapter, we'll explore security governance and risk management. We'll dive into how to establish governance structures, develop risk management processes, and create security policies, standards, and procedures that align with your organisation's goals.

4 Security Governance and Risk Management

Introduction

Security governance isn't just a box-ticking exercise; it's the backbone of your organisation's approach to security. It's about embedding security into the very fabric of your business, ensuring that every decision, process, and strategy aligns with your organisation's goals and risk appetite. In today's rapidly evolving digital landscape, where cyber threats are becoming more sophisticated and regulations stricter, having an effective security governance framework is essential. This framework transforms security from a reactive, IT-focused function into a proactive, business-driven initiative, integrating seamlessly with your corporate governance.

The Role of Security Governance

At its core, security governance is about providing direction and oversight. It's the mechanism by which organisations ensure that their security efforts are aligned with broader business objectives. Effective security governance establishes a framework for accountability, clearly defining roles and responsibilities, and ensuring that security is prioritised at every level. The key objectives of security governance include the following.

Aligning Security with Business Goals

Security efforts must be in sync with your organisation's strategic objectives. This alignment ensures that security investments are

DOI: 10.1201/9781003585923-4

justified and focused on protecting the most critical assets, ultimately turning security into a business enabler rather than a cost burden.

To align security with business goals, organisations must first understand their strategic priorities, whether it's expanding into new markets, protecting intellectual property, or maintaining customer trust. Security initiatives should then be tailored to support these priorities. For example, if customer trust is a key strategic goal, then prioritising data protection measures, particularly around customer data, becomes crucial. This could involve implementing advanced encryption techniques, ensuring compliance with data protection regulations, and establishing robust incident response plans to manage potential breaches.

Proactive Risk Management

One of the primary functions of security governance is to manage risks proactively. Rather than reacting to security incidents after they occur, a proactive risk management approach involves continuously identifying, assessing, and mitigating risks. This approach not only reduces the likelihood of incidents but also limits their potential impact.

Effective risk management requires a deep understanding of the organisation's risk landscape. This includes internal risks, such as outdated systems and human error, as well as external threats, like cyberattacks and natural disasters. Once risks are identified, they must be assessed based on their likelihood and potential impact, allowing organisations to prioritise their response. For instance, a risk assessment might reveal that phishing attacks are a significant threat due to their prevalence and potential to cause data breaches. In response, the organisation could implement email filtering technologies, conduct regular phishing simulations, and provide ongoing training to employees.

Ensuring Regulatory Compliance

In today's environment, compliance with laws and regulations isn't optional, it's mandatory. Organisations operate in a landscape filled with regulatory requirements, such as GDPR, HIPAA, and the Sarbanes-Oxley Act, depending on their industry and location. Security governance ensures that the organisation not only complies with these laws but also stays ahead of changes in the regulatory environment.

This is where Governance, Risk, and Compliance (GRC) comes into play. GRC is an integrated approach that ensures an organisation meets regulatory requirements, manages risks effectively, and governs security practices efficiently. We'll dive deeper into GRC in Chapter 11, but it's important to recognise its relevance here as a framework that helps align security governance with broader compliance and risk management objectives.

Compliance goes beyond simply avoiding penalties; it's about maintaining your organisation's reputation and trust with stakeholders. For example, GDPR imposes strict requirements on how organisations handle personal data, including how they collect, store, and share it. Non-compliance can lead to severe penalties and loss of customer trust. To ensure compliance, organisations need to implement comprehensive data protection policies, regularly audit their practices, and stay informed about changes in regulations. Regular training for employees on regulatory requirements and the implication of non-compliance is also crucial.

Optimising Resources

Security governance plays a critical role in resource optimisation. In many organisations, resources, both financial and human, are limited. Therefore, it's essential to allocate these resources in a way that maximises their impact. By prioritising security initiatives that align with business goals and risk management strategies, organisations can ensure that they are getting the most value out of their investments.

Resource optimisation involves more than just budgeting; it requires strategic thinking. For example, instead of spreading resources thinly across numerous initiatives, a technology company might choose to focus on a few high-impact areas, such as advanced threat detection or securing cloud environments. This focused approach ensures that the organisation's most valuable assets are well-protected and that security efforts contribute directly to business success.

Measuring and Improving Performance

You can't manage what you don't measure. Security governance provides a framework for setting and tracking Key Performance Indicators (KPIs) that reflect the effectiveness of your security initiatives. Regularly reviewing these KPIs allows organisations to identify areas for improvement and adjust their strategies accordingly.

Performance measurement in security is not just about counting incidents or compliance checks; it's about understanding the effectiveness of your overall security posture. For example, an organisation might track metrics such as the average time to detect and respond to security incidents, the number of systems fully patched within required timeframes, or employee adherence to security policies. These metrics provide insight into how well the organisation is managing its security risks and where additional resources or attention might be needed.

Building a Security Governance Framework

Creating an effective security governance framework is a complex task that requires careful planning and ongoing management. This framework should be tailored to your organisation's specific needs, taking into account its size, industry, and risk profile. The key components of a strong security governance framework include the following.

Security Policies, Standards, and Procedures

These elements form the foundation of your security governance framework. Policies provide high-level direction, setting out the organisation's security objectives and the principles that guide decision-making. Standards offer more detailed guidance on how to achieve these objectives, specifying the technologies, processes, and practices that should be used. Procedures are step-by-step instructions that ensure policies and standards are implemented effectively.

It's important to regularly review and update these documents to reflect changes in the threat landscape, technological advancements, and regulatory requirements. For example, as more organisations move to cloud-based environments, security policies may need to be updated to address specific risks associated with cloud computing, such as data breaches and service disruptions.

Clear Roles, Responsibilities, and Accountability

A clear definition of roles and responsibilities is essential for effective security governance. This involves not just assigning tasks but also ensuring that everyone in the organisation understands their role in maintaining security. From the CISO to individual employees, everyone has a part to play.

Accountability is also crucial. When security responsibilities are clearly defined, it's easier to hold individuals and teams accountable for their actions, or inactions. For instance, if a data breach occurs due to a failure to apply a critical patch, it should be clear who was responsible for the patch management process and where the breakdown occurred. This clarity helps in addressing the issue and preventing future incidents.

Security Committees and Councils

Establishing a security committee or council can provide valuable oversight and strategic direction. These groups typically include senior executives, IT leaders, and representatives from key business units. Their role is to ensure that security is integrated into the organisation's overall strategy and that decisions are made with a comprehensive understanding of the risks and benefits.

Security committees are particularly useful in large organisations, where the complexity of the environment requires coordination across multiple departments and regions. Regular meetings of the security committee provide an opportunity to review the organisation's security posture, discuss emerging threats, and approve new initiatives. This ensures that security remains a top priority at the highest levels of the organisation.

A Risk Management Framework

A well-defined risk management framework is crucial for identifying, assessing, and mitigating risks. This framework should be integrated into the broader security governance structure, ensuring that risks are managed consistently and transparently across the organisation.

A comprehensive risk management framework typically includes risk assessments, risk registers, and mitigation strategies. Risk assessments help identify potential threats and vulnerabilities, while the risk register tracks these risks over time, along with the controls in place to mitigate them. Mitigation strategies are then developed to address the most critical risks, ensuring that resources are allocated where they are needed most.

Compliance and Regulatory Oversight

Ensuring compliance with relevant laws, regulations, and industry standards is a key responsibility of security governance. This involves not only implementing the necessary controls but also regularly auditing these controls to ensure they are effective.

As part of a comprehensive GRC strategy, compliance oversight should be proactive rather than reactive. This means staying ahead of regulatory changes and adjusting your security practices accordingly. For example, if new data protection regulations are introduced in your industry, your organisation should be ready to comply from day one, rather than scrambling to meet the requirements after the fact. Regular audits and assessments are essential to maintaining compliance and avoiding potential fines or other penalties.

Security Awareness and Training

Building a culture of security within your organisation requires ongoing education and awareness efforts. Security governance should include a structured programme for training employees at all levels, raising awareness of security threats, and promoting best practices.

A strong security awareness programme doesn't just teach employees about the latest threats; it also helps them understand their role in protecting the organisation's assets. This might include training on how to recognise phishing emails, the importance of using strong passwords, and the procedures to follow in the event of a security incident. Regular training sessions, combined with ongoing communications such as newsletters and alerts, help keep security top-of-mind for employees.

Performance Metrics and Reporting

To measure the effectiveness of your security governance framework, you need to establish Key Performance Indicators (KPIs) and regularly report on security performance. This might include metrics such as the number of security incidents, the time taken to respond to incidents, or the level of compliance with security policies.

Regular reporting on these metrics to senior leadership helps ensure that security remains a priority at the highest levels of the organisation. It also provides the information needed to make informed decisions about where to allocate resources and how to improve security practices.

Establishing Your Governance Framework

Implementing a security governance framework is a multi-step process that requires careful planning and execution. Here's how to get started:

Engage Senior Leadership

Security governance must be driven from the top. Engage senior leaders early in the process, ensuring they understand the importance of security and are committed to supporting governance initiatives. Leadership buy-in is essential for securing the resources and authority needed to implement effective security governance.

Define Security Objectives and Policies

Start by clearly defining your organisation's security objectives and developing policies that align with these goals. These policies should be comprehensive, covering all aspects of your organisation's operations, from data protection to incident response. They serve as the foundation for your security efforts, guiding decisions and actions across the organisation.

Assign Roles and Responsibilities

Clearly assign roles and responsibilities to ensure everyone in the organisation understands their part in maintaining security. This includes not only the security team but also business units, IT departments, and individual employees. Clear definitions help ensure that everyone knows what is expected of them and can be held accountable.

Implement a Risk Management Framework

Develop and implement a risk management framework that includes processes for identifying, assessing, and mitigating risks. This framework should be integrated into the broader security governance structure to ensure consistent risk management across the organisation.

Develop a Compliance and Audit Programme

Establish a programme for monitoring compliance with security policies and regulatory requirements. This should include regular audits, both internal and external, to identify gaps and ensure that your organisation remains compliant.

Promote Security Awareness and Training

Implement a comprehensive training programme that educates employees about security threats, best practices, and their role in maintaining security. Regular training, combined with ongoing communications, helps build a culture of security throughout the organisation.

Monitor and Report on Security Performance

Establish metrics for measuring the effectiveness of your security governance framework and regularly report on security performance to senior leadership. This ensures that security remains a priority and that your security efforts are continuously improved.

Understanding Risk Management

Risk management is a critical component of security governance, focusing on identifying, assessing, and mitigating risks to your organisation's assets. A robust risk management process involves several key steps.

Risk Identification

The first step in the risk management process is to identify potential risks to your organisation's assets. These might include cyber threats such as hacking and phishing, as well as internal risks like human error and system failures. The goal is to develop a comprehensive understanding of the threats facing your organisation.

Risk Assessment

Once risks have been identified, the next step is to assess their likelihood and potential impact. This involves evaluating the probability of each risk occurring and the potential damage it could cause. Risks are then prioritised based on this assessment, allowing the organisation to focus its resources on the most significant threats.

Risk Mitigation

After assessing the risks, the next step is to develop and implement controls to mitigate them. This might involve implementing technical controls, such as firewalls or encryption, as well as organisational controls, such as security policies and training programmes. The goal is to reduce the likelihood of the risk occurring and minimise its impact if it does.

Risk Monitoring and Review

Risk management is an ongoing process. Organisations must continuously monitor their risk environment, reviewing and updating controls as necessary to ensure they remain effective. This includes conducting regular risk assessments, tracking the effectiveness of mitigation strategies, and adjusting controls in response to new threats or changes in the business environment.

Types of Security Risks

Security risks can be broadly categorised into several types, each requiring different approaches to mitigation.

Cyber Risks

These are risks associated with cyber threats such as hacking, phishing, ransomware, and other forms of cyberattacks. Cyber risks are often the most visible and high-profile security risks, and they require robust technical controls and incident response capabilities.

Operational Risks

Operational risks arise from the day-to-day operations of the organisation. These might include risks associated with system failures, human error, or process breakdowns. Operational risks can have a significant impact on business continuity and require effective monitoring and response strategies.

Compliance Risks

Compliance risks arise from the potential for non-compliance with laws, regulations, and industry standards. These risks can result in legal penalties, financial losses, and damage to the organisation's reputation. Compliance risks require ongoing monitoring and regular audits to ensure that the organisation remains compliant with all relevant requirements.

Reputational Risks

Reputational risks arise from events or actions that could damage the organisation's reputation. These might include security breaches, data leaks, or unethical behaviour. Reputational risks can have long-lasting effects on customer trust and require proactive communication and crisis management strategies.

Strategic Risks

Strategic risks arise from decisions that could affect the long-term success of the organisation. These might include risks associated with mergers and acquisitions, entering new markets, or adopting new technologies. Strategic risks require careful planning and decision-making to ensure that security considerations are integrated into the organisation's strategic goals.

Integrating Risk Management into Governance

For risk management to be effective, it must be fully integrated into the broader security governance framework. This integration ensures that risk management is not a standalone activity but a core part of the organisation's security strategy. Steps for integration include the following.

Align Risk Management with Business Goals

Ensure that risk management activities are aligned with the organisation's strategic objectives. This involves identifying the key risks that could impact the organisation's ability to achieve its goals and prioritising those risks accordingly.

Embed Risk Management in Decision-Making

Make risk management a key part of decision-making processes across the organisation. This involves incorporating risk assessments into strategic planning, project management, and day-to-day operations.

Foster a Risk-Aware Culture

Promote a culture of risk awareness across the organisation, ensuring that employees at all levels understand the importance of risk management and their role in identifying and mitigating risks.

Establish Clear Reporting and Accountability Structures

Ensure that there are clear reporting and accountability structures for risk management. This includes defining who is responsible for managing risks, how risks are reported, and how risk management activities are monitored and reviewed.

Regularly Review and Update Risk Management Practices

Risk management is not a one-time activity. Regularly review and update risk management practices to ensure they remain effective in the face of evolving threats and changing business conditions.

Conclusion

Security governance and risk management are critical components of a robust enterprise security architecture. By establishing a comprehensive security governance framework and integrating risk management into decision-making processes, organisations can ensure that their security efforts are aligned with business goals, risks are managed effectively, and compliance requirements are met.

In the next chapter, we'll explore the building blocks of security architecture, including Identity and Access Management (IAM), network security, application security, data security, and cloud security. These components are essential for protecting your organisation's assets and ensuring a strong security posture.

5
Building Blocks of Security Architecture

Introduction to Security Architecture

Security architecture is the foundation upon which an organisation's security posture is built. It involves designing and implementing the various components, systems, and processes that work together to protect the organisation's information and assets. Think of it as the blueprint for how security is integrated into every aspect of your business.

An effective security architecture doesn't just protect against threats; it enables the organisation to operate confidently in an increasingly digital world. It ensures that security measures are robust, comprehensive, aligned with business objectives, and adaptable to changing risks.

In this chapter, we'll explore the core building blocks of security architecture, covering essential areas such as Identity and Access Management (IAM), network security, application security, data security, and cloud security. These components form the backbone of your security strategy, ensuring that every part of your organisation is protected against a wide range of threats.

Identity and Access Management (IAM)

Identity and Access Management (IAM) is a critical component of security architecture. It ensures that the right people (or systems) have access to the right resources at the right times, for the right reasons. IAM controls who can access your organisation's resources, what they can do with that access, and how their activities are tracked and monitored (Figure 5.1).

DOI: 10.1201/9781003585923-5

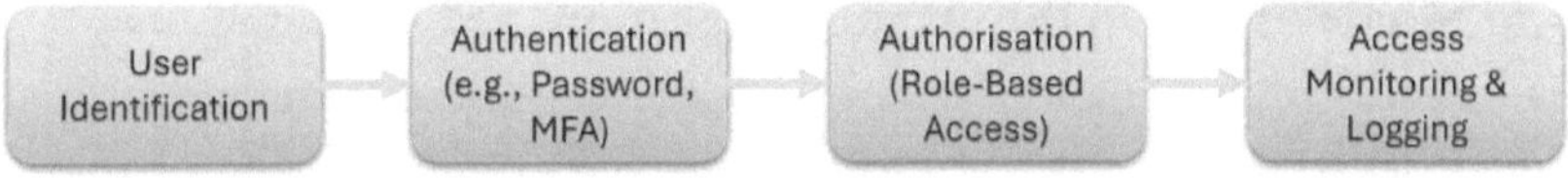

Figure 5.1 IAM process – flowchart of user identification, authentication, authorisation, and access monitoring.

IAM Strategy and Planning

Developing an IAM strategy is essential for aligning IAM initiatives with organisational goals. This includes planning for future growth, integrating IAM with existing systems, and selecting technologies that support long-term security needs. A well-defined strategy ensures that IAM not only secures access but also supports business operations efficiently.

Key Concepts in IAM

1. **Identification and Authentication:** This process verifies the identity of users or systems before granting access to resources. Authentication methods can range from simple passwords to more advanced methods like Multi-Factor Authentication (MFA) or biometric verification.
2. **Authorisation:** After authentication, authorisation determines what resources users can access and what actions they can perform. Typically managed through roles and permissions, authorisation ensures that users only access the information necessary for their job functions.
3. **User Provisioning and Deprovisioning:** Provisioning involves creating user accounts and assigning access rights, while deprovisioning revokes access when it's no longer needed. Automating these processes is crucial for maintaining security by ensuring timely updates to user access based on role changes or employee departures.
4. **Privileged Access Management (PAM):** PAM manages and monitors privileged accounts with elevated access rights. Controlling and auditing these accounts is critical since they are often targeted by attackers due to their powerful capabilities.

5. **Single Sign-On (SSO) and Federation:** SSO allows users to access multiple applications with one set of credentials, while federation extends SSO to external systems. These tools simplify access management and enhance security by reducing the number of passwords users need to manage.
6. **Access Governance:** Regular reviews and audits of access rights are necessary to ensure users have only the permissions they need, preventing privilege creep and reducing the risk of insider threats.

IAM Lifecycle Management

IAM isn't a one-time implementation but a continuous process that evolves with your organisation. This includes user onboarding, role changes, and offboarding. Ensuring these processes are seamless, secure, and auditable is critical, and automation can play a key role in managing them efficiently.

Access Review and Certification

Periodic access reviews and certification are essential for maintaining a secure environment. Automated tools can facilitate these reviews, but manual oversight is often necessary for handling exceptions and anomalies. Regular reviews help maintain alignment between user roles and their access rights.

Challenges in IAM

- **Complexity:** Managing access across a large, diverse organisation can be challenging, especially when integrating with legacy systems or third-party applications.
- **User Experience:** Balancing security with usability is a constant challenge, as strong authentication measures can sometimes frustrate users.
- **Scalability:** As organisations grow, their IAM systems must scale to support an increasing number of users, applications, and devices.

Best Practices for IAM

- **Adopt a Zero Trust Approach:** Implement a Zero Trust model where no one is trusted by default, regardless of their location, requiring continuous verification of user identities and access requests.
- **Implement Multi-Factor Authentication (MFA):** MFA adds an extra layer of security, significantly reducing the risk of compromised credentials.
- **Regularly Review Access Rights:** Conduct regular access reviews to ensure that users only have access to the resources they need, preventing privilege creep.
- **Use Role-Based Access Control (RBAC):** Assign permissions based on roles rather than individuals, simplifying access management and ensuring appropriate levels of access.
- **Monitor and Audit Access Activities:** Implement logging and monitoring to track access activities, particularly for privileged accounts, and regularly review audit logs for suspicious behaviour.

Network Security

Network security is another critical building block of security architecture (Figure 5.2). It involves protecting the organisation's network infrastructure from threats such as unauthorised access, data breaches, and cyberattacks. A secure network is essential for safeguarding the organisation's data and ensuring the integrity and availability of its systems. Figure 5.2 shows a simplified structure for key areas of consideration for network security.

Network Security Architectures

Different network security architectures, such as perimeter-based security and Zero Trust architectures, offer various approaches to securing an organisation's network. Perimeter-based security focuses on protecting the network's boundaries, while Zero Trust assumes that threats can originate both inside and outside the network, requiring continuous verification of all access requests.

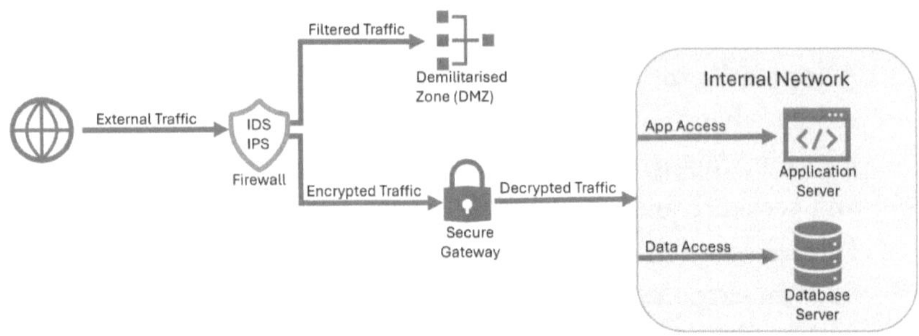

Figure 5.2 Network security architecture – flow of traffic through firewall, DMZ, IDS/IPS, and secure gateway to secure internal networks.

Network segmentation is a key strategy within these architectures, dividing the network into isolated segments, each with its own security controls. This approach limits the spread of threats, ensuring that a breach in one segment doesn't compromise the entire network.

Key Concepts in Network Security

- **Firewalls:** Firewalls are the first line of defence in network security, monitoring and controlling incoming and outgoing traffic based on predetermined security rules.
- **Intrusion Detection and Prevention Systems (IDS/IPS):** IDS and IPS detect and prevent malicious activities on the network. IDS monitors traffic for suspicious behaviour, while IPS blocks or mitigates threats in real time.
- **Virtual Private Networks (VPNs):** VPNs create secure, encrypted connections over public networks, allowing remote users to access the organisation's resources securely.
- **Network Segmentation:** Dividing the network into smaller, isolated segments with their own security controls limits the spread of malware or other threats within the network.
- **Zero Trust Network Architecture (ZTNA):** ZTNA requires all users and devices to be authenticated and authorised before accessing any resources, regardless of their location within or outside the network.
- **Network Access Control (NAC):** NAC enforces security policies at the network entry point, ensuring that only

authorised devices with compliant configurations are allowed to connect.

Advanced Network Threats and Mitigation Strategies

As network threats evolve, organisations must stay vigilant against Advanced Persistent Threats (APTs) and Distributed Denial of Service (DDoS) attacks. APTs often involve prolonged, targeted attacks aimed at stealing sensitive data, while DDoS attacks aim to disrupt services by overwhelming network resources. Mitigating these threats requires advanced detection tools, such as AI and machine learning, to identify patterns and respond to anomalies.

Challenges in Network Security

- **Evolving Threats:** Network security threats are constantly evolving, requiring organisations to stay vigilant and continuously update their defences.
- **Complexity:** Securing a large, complex network with a mix of legacy systems, cloud environments, and mobile devices can be challenging.
- **Performance vs Security:** Strong security controls can impact network performance, requiring a careful balance between security and usability.

Best Practices for Network Security

- **Implement Defence in Depth:** Use multiple layers of security controls to protect the network from different types of threats.
- **Regularly Update and Patch Systems:** Keep network devices and systems up to date with the latest security patches to protect against known vulnerabilities.
- **Monitor Network Traffic:** Continuously monitor network traffic for signs of suspicious behaviour using tools such as IDS/IPS and SIEM.

- **Enforce Network Segmentation:** Segment the network to limit the spread of threats, using VLANs, firewalls, and Access Control Lists (ACLs).
- **Adopt a Zero Trust Approach:** Continuously verify all users and devices before granting access to network resources, reducing the risk of unauthorised access.

Application Security

Application security focuses on protecting software applications from threats such as code injection, cross-site scripting (XSS), and other vulnerabilities. As more organisations rely on custom-built and third-party applications, ensuring the security of these applications is increasingly important.

Secure Software Development Lifecycle (SDLC)

Integrating security into every stage of the Software Development Lifecycle (SDLC) is critical. This approach ensures that security considerations are embedded from the design phase through to deployment, reducing the likelihood of vulnerabilities being introduced into the final product.

Key Concepts in Application Security

- **Static and Dynamic Application Security Testing (SAST/DAST):** SAST analyses source code for vulnerabilities, while DAST tests the application in its running state to identify potential weaknesses.
- **Web Application Firewalls (WAFs):** WAFs protect web applications by filtering and monitoring HTTP traffic, blocking malicious traffic before it reaches the application.
- **Application Security Testing (AST):** Regular testing of applications for vulnerabilities, such as weak authentication or insecure data storage, helps ensure that security is maintained throughout the application's lifecycle.

- **Threat Modelling:** Identifying potential threats to an application and designing countermeasures to mitigate them helps prioritise security efforts.
- **Secure Coding Practices:** Writing code that is free from common vulnerabilities reduces the risk of security flaws in applications.

Software Supply Chain Security

Securing the software supply chain is increasingly important, especially when using third-party components or open-source libraries. Best practices include vetting third-party software, managing dependencies carefully, and ensuring that all components are secure and up to date.

DevSecOps Integration

Integrating security into DevOps practices (DevSecOps) ensures that security is considered throughout the development and deployment process. This includes automated security testing in Continuous Integration and Continuous Deployment (CI/CD) pipelines, as well as fostering collaboration between development, operations, and security teams.

Challenges in Application Security

- **Complexity:** Securing complex applications with multiple components and dependencies is challenging, especially when dealing with third-party libraries.
- **Speed of Development:** The pressure to release software quickly can lead to shortcuts in security, resulting in vulnerabilities.
- **Integration with Development Processes:** Integrating security into agile and DevOps processes can be difficult, especially when development teams focus on speed and innovation.

Best Practices for Application Security

- **Implement a Secure SDLC:** Integrate security into every stage of the software development lifecycle.
- **Conduct Regular Security Testing:** Use automated tools to perform regular security testing, including SAST, DAST, and AST.
- **Adopt Secure Coding Practices:** Educate developers on secure coding practices and provide guidelines for writing secure code.
- **Use Web Application Firewalls (WAFs):** Deploy WAFs to protect web applications from common attacks.
- **Conduct Threat Modelling:** Regularly perform threat modelling to identify and mitigate potential threats.

Data Security

Data security involves protecting the organisation's data from unauthorised access, alteration, or destruction. With the increasing value of data and growing regulatory requirements, data security has become a top priority for organisations.

Data Security Governance

Establishing strong data security governance is essential for ensuring that data protection efforts are consistent and aligned with broader Governance, Risk, and Compliance (GRC) initiatives. This includes developing policies and procedures that cover the entire data lifecycle, from creation to disposal.

Key Concepts in Data Security

- **Data Classification:** Categorising data based on its sensitivity and importance helps determine the appropriate security controls.
- **Data Encryption:** Encrypting data both at rest and in transit ensures that even if data is intercepted or stolen, it cannot be read without the encryption key.

- **Data Masking:** Replacing sensitive data with fictional data for non-production environments protects against unauthorised access during development and testing.
- **Data Loss Prevention (DLP):** DLP solutions monitor and control the movement of data, preventing unauthorised sharing or leakage.
- **Access Controls:** Restricting who can access specific data and what actions they can perform ensures that only authorised users have access to sensitive information.
- **Data Retention and Disposal:** Securely deleting data when it is no longer needed reduces the risk of data breaches and ensures compliance with regulations.

Data Sovereignty and Compliance

Data sovereignty challenges are particularly significant for multinational organisations. Navigating the different regulatory requirements across jurisdictions requires careful planning and robust data security controls to ensure compliance while protecting sensitive information.

Data Protection in the Cloud

Securing data in cloud environments presents unique challenges. Organisations must ensure that their data protection strategies include strong encryption, secure key management, and adherence to the shared responsibility model, where both the cloud provider and the customer share responsibility for security.

Challenges in Data Security

- **Volume of Data:** Managing and securing large volumes of data can be challenging.
- **Regulatory Compliance:** Ensuring compliance with data protection regulations requires ongoing monitoring and audits.
- **Data Access:** Balancing accessibility with security can be difficult in organisations with diverse user groups.

Best Practices for Data Security

- **Classify and Protect Data:** Implement a data classification scheme and apply appropriate security controls based on the classification.
- **Encrypt Sensitive Data:** Use encryption to protect data both at rest and in transit.
- **Implement Data Loss Prevention (DLP) Tools:** Deploy DLP tools to monitor and control the movement of sensitive data.
- **Use Data Masking for Non-production Environments:** Apply data masking in non-production environments to protect sensitive data.
- **Establish Data Retention and Disposal Policies:** Develop and enforce data retention and disposal policies to securely delete data when no longer needed.

Cloud Security

As organisations increasingly adopt cloud computing, securing cloud environments has become a critical component of security architecture. Cloud security involves protecting data, applications, and infrastructure in cloud environments from threats such as data breaches, unauthorised access, and service disruptions. Figure 5.3 shows a very high level and simplified view of cloud security.

Cloud Security Architectures

Cloud environments vary widely, from public to private to hybrid clouds. Each requires a tailored security approach. Public clouds might focus on securing data and access through encryption and IAM, while private clouds could emphasise network security and compliance controls. Hybrid clouds require a combination of strategies to manage the complexities of multiple environments.

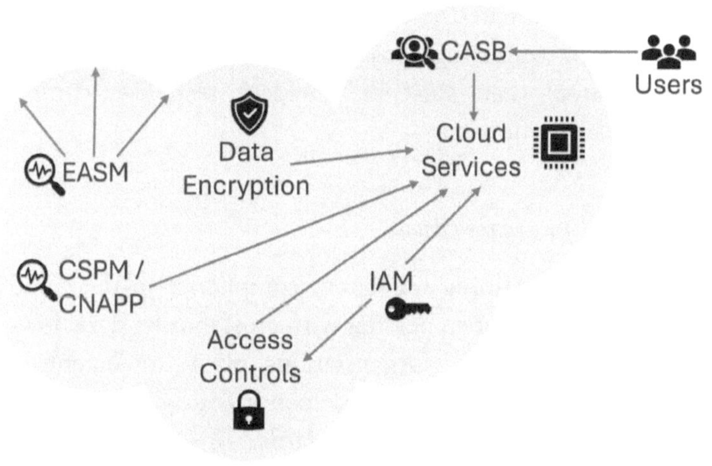

Figure 5.3 Simplified example of cloud security controls.

Key Concepts in Cloud Security

- **Shared Responsibility Model:** In the cloud, security is shared between the Cloud Service Provider (CSP) and the customer, with the CSP securing the infrastructure and the customer securing their data and applications.
- **Cloud Identity and Access Management (IAM):** Cloud IAM provides granular access control to cloud resources, ensuring that only authorised users can access specific services and data.
- **Cloud Encryption:** Encrypting data in the cloud, both at rest and in transit, is essential for protecting sensitive information.
- **Cloud Security Posture Management (CSPM):** CSPM tools monitor cloud environments for misconfigurations, identify security risks, and enforce best practices for cloud security.
- **Cloud Data Loss Prevention (DLP):** Cloud DLP solutions help prevent the unauthorised sharing or leakage of sensitive data in cloud environments.

Cloud Security Automation and Orchestration

Automation and orchestration are vital for managing security in dynamic cloud environments. Infrastructure as Code (IaC) allows organisations to automate the deployment and management of security configurations, ensuring consistency and reducing human error. Orchestration tools can automate incident response, compliance checks, and security updates.

Regulatory Compliance in the Cloud

Achieving and maintaining regulatory compliance in the cloud can be complex, especially when dealing with cross-border data flows and multi-cloud environments. Organisations must implement robust data governance, monitor compliance continuously, and ensure that all cloud services meet regulatory standards.

Challenges in Cloud Security

- **Complexity of Cloud Environments:** Managing security across complex cloud environments with multiple services and configurations can be challenging.
- **Visibility:** Gaining visibility into cloud environments, particularly in multi-cloud or hybrid deployments, can be difficult.
- **Compliance:** Ensuring compliance with regulatory requirements in the cloud requires careful management of data and security controls.

Best Practices for Cloud Security

- **Understand the Shared Responsibility Model:** Clearly define security responsibilities between the cloud service provider and the customer.
- **Implement Cloud IAM:** Use cloud IAM solutions to enforce granular access controls and manage access to cloud resources.
- **Encrypt Data in the Cloud:** Encrypt sensitive data in the cloud and manage encryption keys securely.
- **Use Cloud Security Posture Management (CSPM) Tools:** Deploy CSPM tools to monitor cloud environments and enforce security best practices.

- **Conduct Regular Cloud Security Assessments:** Regularly assess cloud environments for vulnerabilities and ensure that security controls are effective.

Conclusion

The building blocks of security architecture, Identity and Access Management (IAM), network security, application security, data security, and cloud security, are essential for protecting an organisation's assets and ensuring a strong security posture. By understanding and implementing these components, organisations can build a robust security architecture that aligns with business objectives, adapts to changing threats, and protects against a wide range of risks.

In the next chapter, we'll explore how to design security architectures that integrate these building blocks into a cohesive and effective security strategy. We'll discuss the principles of security architecture design, how to tailor security solutions to different environments, and how to scale your architecture as your organisation grows.

6 DESIGNING SECURITY ARCHITECTURES

Introduction to Security Architecture Design

Designing a security architecture is a critical and complex endeavour that underpins an organisation's ability to protect its assets while advancing its business objectives. This process goes far beyond simply implementing technical controls; it involves constructing a comprehensive and resilient framework that can adapt to emerging threats, scale with organisational growth, and integrate seamlessly with existing processes and technologies.

A robust security architecture must be aligned with the organisation's goals, thoroughly address its risk landscape, comply with regulatory requirements, and be adaptable to its technological environment. This requires not just technical expertise but also strategic insight and collaboration across departments. The resulting architecture serves as a foundation that enables the organisation to operate securely and efficiently, fostering innovation and growth while maintaining a strong security posture.

In this chapter, we'll delve deeply into the fundamental principles of security architecture design, outline the detailed steps involved in building a resilient security architecture, and discuss the specific considerations needed for tailoring security solutions to different environments. We'll also explore how to effectively scale security architectures as organisations expand, and how to ensure that your design remains robust and adaptive in the face of evolving threats.

DOI: 10.1201/9781003585923-6

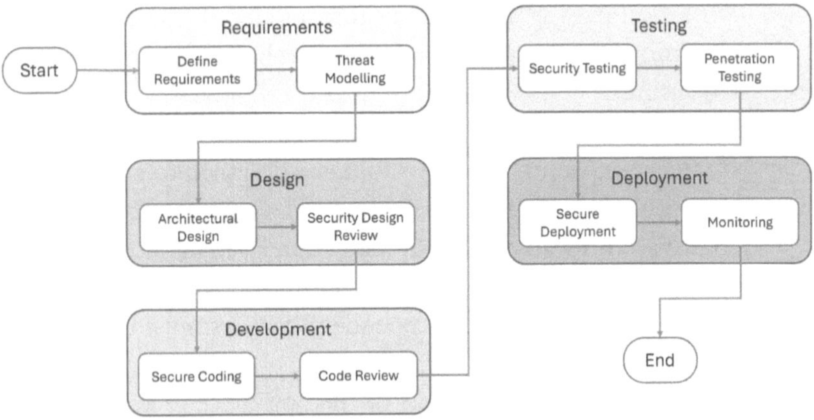

Figure 6.1 Diagram illustrating security by design principles integrated into each stage of the system design process.

Principles of Security Architecture Design

Designing a security architecture is guided by several core principles that ensure the architecture is resilient, adaptable, and aligned with the organisation's needs . These principles form the bedrock of decision-making during the the full lifecycle of the definition through design and deployment processes (Figure 6.1), helping to balance security requirements with usability, performance, and cost.

Key Principles

- **Defence in Depth:** This principle is based on the concept of layered security, where multiple, redundant security controls are implemented across the architecture to protect against threats. The idea is that if one layer is breached, others remain to safeguard the system. This approach mitigates the risk of any single point of failure compromising the entire system.
  - **Comprehensive Implementation:** Defence in depth can be achieved through a combination of physical, technical, and administrative controls. Physical controls might include secured access to data centres, while technical controls encompass firewalls, Intrusion Detection/Prevention Systems (IDPS), and endpoint security. Administrative controls, such as security policies and procedures, provide

the overarching governance that guides the implementation and management of these technical and physical measures.

- **Resilience through Redundancy:** Each layer in a defence-in-depth strategy should be designed to provide a fallback if others fail. For instance, if an attacker bypasses network firewalls, endpoint detection systems should still be able to detect and mitigate the threat. This redundancy ensures that multiple, independent barriers must be overcome for an attack to succeed.

- **Least Privilege:** The principle of least privilege dictates that users and systems should only have the minimum access necessary to perform their functions. By limiting access to the least amount of resources required, this approach reduces the risk of misuse, whether accidental or intentional, and limits the potential damage from compromised accounts.
    - **Granular Access Controls:** Implementing least privilege requires granular access controls that are carefully aligned with job functions and roles. Role-Based Access Control (RBAC) is commonly used to enforce this principle, where access rights are tied to the responsibilities of a particular role within the organisation. This ensures that users only have access to the information and systems necessary for their duties.
    - **Dynamic Privilege Management:** As roles within an organisation evolve, so too must the access rights associated with them. Dynamic privilege management involves regularly reviewing and adjusting access rights as job roles change or as users' responsibilities expand or contract. This ongoing adjustment helps maintain a strict alignment between access rights and operational needs, reducing the risk of privilege creep.
- **Segmentation and Isolation:** Network segmentation involves dividing the network into smaller, isolated segments, each with its own security controls. This compartmentalisation limits the potential spread of threats within the network and makes it more difficult for attackers to move laterally across the system.

  - **Isolating Sensitive Systems:** Critical systems, such as those handling payment processing or sensitive personal data, should be isolated from the broader network. This can be achieved through the use of Virtual Local Area Networks (VLANs) or by physically separating systems with firewalls that restrict communication between different network segments.
  - **Minimising Attack Surfaces:** By isolating different parts of the network, the attack surface is effectively reduced. Attackers who gain access to one segment are contained within it, preventing them from easily reaching other parts of the network. This segmentation is especially crucial in protecting high-value targets within an organisation, such as customer databases or financial systems.
- **Security by Design:** Security should be integrated into the design of systems and applications from the outset, ensuring that it is a foundational element rather than an afterthought. This principle ensures that security considerations are embedded into every layer of the architecture and that potential vulnerabilities are addressed early in the design process.
  - **Secure Development Lifecycle:** Implementing security by design often involves adopting a Secure software Development Lifecycle (SDLC). This includes incorporating security into the initial design phase, performing threat modelling, conducting secure coding practices, and conducting regular security testing throughout the development process.
  - **Proactive Threat Management:** By considering security from the beginning, organisations can proactively manage potential threats rather than reactively addressing vulnerabilities after they have been discovered. This proactive approach not only improves the overall security posture but also reduces the cost and complexity of implementing security controls later in the development cycle.
- **Scalability and Flexibility:** The security architecture should be designed to scale with the organisation as it grows and evolves. It should also be flexible enough to adapt to changes

in the threat landscape, regulatory requirements, and technological advancements.

  - **Modular Design:** A modular approach to security architecture allows for components to be added, removed, or upgraded without disrupting the entire system. This flexibility is crucial for organisations that are rapidly expanding or that frequently integrate new technologies into their operations.
  - **Elastic Security Solutions:** In cloud environments, security solutions need to be elastic, scaling up or down in response to changing workloads. Automated scaling mechanisms, combined with cloud-native security tools, can help organisations maintain a strong security posture even as their operational demands fluctuate.

- **Resilience and Recovery:** The architecture must be designed to withstand and recover from security incidents. This includes incorporating redundancy, failover mechanisms, and disaster recovery plans to ensure business continuity even in the event of an attack or system failure.
  - **Disaster Recovery Planning:** Effective disaster recovery planning involves identifying critical business processes, determining acceptable downtime, and implementing backup and recovery solutions that can quickly restore operations. Regular testing of disaster recovery plans is essential to ensure they work as intended in the event of an actual incident.
  - **Building in Redundancy:** Redundancy should be built into the architecture at multiple levels, including data redundancy through backups, system redundancy through failover servers, and network redundancy through multiple Internet Service Providers (ISPs). These redundancies ensure that if one component fails, another can take its place without significant disruption.
- **User-Centred Security:** Security measures should be designed with the user in mind, ensuring they are user-friendly and do not hinder productivity. When security controls are cumbersome or obstructive, users are more likely to circumvent them, weakening the overall security posture.

  - **Balancing Usability and Security:** Finding the right balance between usability and security is critical. Security mechanisms should be strong enough to protect the system, but not so onerous that they disrupt users' workflows or lead to poor user experience. User-centred design principles help ensure that security controls are integrated seamlessly into users' daily activities.
  - **Training and Awareness:** A user-centred approach also involves educating users about security best practices and the importance of compliance. Regular training sessions and awareness programmes help build a culture of security within the organisation, where users understand their role in protecting the organisation's assets.
- **Continuous Monitoring and Improvement:** Security architecture design is not a one-time activity. The architecture should be continuously monitored, assessed, and improved to address emerging threats and changing business needs. Regular reviews and updates help ensure that the architecture remains effective and responsive to new challenges.
  - **Real-Time Threat Detection:** Continuous monitoring involves using tools like Security Information and Event Management (SIEM) systems to collect and analyse data in real time, identifying and responding to potential threats as they arise. This proactive approach helps prevent incidents before they escalate into full-blown security breaches.
  - **Iterative Security Improvements:** As new threats emerge and the organisation's needs evolve, the security architecture must be periodically reviewed and updated. This iterative process ensures that the architecture stays relevant and effective, incorporating the latest security best practices and technologies.

Steps in Designing a Security Architecture

Designing a security architecture is a structured process that ensures all aspects of the organisation's security needs are addressed. The following steps outline the key stages in developing a robust and effective security architecture.

Step 1: Understand Business Objectives and Requirements

The first step is to thoroughly understand the organisation's business objectives, risk appetite, and regulatory requirements. Engaging with key stakeholders across the organisation helps identify the goals and security challenges that the architecture must address.

- **Stakeholder Engagement:** Successful security architecture design begins with understanding the needs and concerns of various stakeholders, including executive leadership, IT, legal, compliance, and business units. Each group brings unique perspectives on what assets need protection, the risks they face, and the regulatory requirements that must be met.
- **Aligning Security with Business Goals:** Security measures should be aligned with the organisation's strategic objectives. For instance, if a primary goal is to expand into new markets, the security architecture must support this growth by ensuring that new systems and processes are secure from the outset.

Step 2: Conduct a Risk Assessment

A comprehensive risk assessment identifies the threats and vulnerabilities that the security architecture must mitigate. This assessment should consider both internal and external threats, evaluate their likelihood, and assess the potential impact on the organisation.

- **Identifying Threats:** The risk assessment process begins by identifying potential threats to the organisation's assets. These threats could be external, such as cyberattacks or natural disasters, or internal, such as insider threats or system failures.
- **Evaluating Vulnerabilities:** Once threats are identified, the next step is to evaluate the vulnerabilities that could be exploited. This involves assessing the organisation's existing security controls, identifying gaps or weaknesses, and determining how these vulnerabilities could be exploited.

- **Assessing Impact:** Finally, the risk assessment evaluates the potential impact of each identified threat. This includes considering the financial, operational, and reputational consequences of a security incident, helping to prioritise which risks need the most urgent attention.

Step 3: Define Security Requirements

Based on the risk assessment, the specific security requirements that the architecture must meet should be clearly defined. These requirements must align with the organisation's business objectives and regulatory obligations while addressing the identified risks.

- **Translating Risks into Requirements:** Security requirements should directly address the risks identified during the assessment. For example, if data breaches are a significant concern, requirements might include strong encryption, access controls, and real-time monitoring.
- **Regulatory Compliance:** Security requirements must also ensure compliance with relevant laws and regulations. This might involve implementing controls to protect Personally Identifiable Information (PII) under GDPR, or ensuring data integrity and availability as required by industry standards like ISO/IEC 27001.

Step 4: Design the Security Architecture

With the security requirements established, the architecture is designed by selecting appropriate security controls, technologies, and processes. This phase incorporates the core principles of security architecture, ensuring a balanced, layered, and scalable design.

- **Selecting Security Controls:** Based on the defined security requirements, select the appropriate controls to protect the organisation's assets. This includes both preventive measures, such as firewalls and encryption, and detective measures, such as Intrusion Detection Systems (IDS) and monitoring tools.
- **Designing for Integration:** The security architecture must integrate seamlessly with the organisation's existing systems

and processes. This requires careful planning to ensure that new security controls do not disrupt operations or create unnecessary complexity.

- **Documenting the Design:** A detailed architectural blueprint should be created, documenting the design and the rationale behind each decision. This blueprint serves as a guide for implementation and a reference for future reviews and updates.

Step 5: Implement the Security Architecture

Implementation involves deploying the selected technologies, configuring security controls, and establishing the necessary processes and procedures. This phase should be conducted methodically, with ongoing testing to ensure that each component functions as intended.

- **Phased Deployment:** Implementation should be phased, starting with critical systems and gradually expanding to cover the entire organisation. This approach allows for testing and adjustments before full-scale deployment, reducing the risk of disruption.
- **Testing and Validation:** Throughout the implementation process, security controls should be thoroughly tested to ensure they meet the defined requirements. This includes functional testing to verify that controls work as expected and stress testing to assess their performance under load.
- **Training and Documentation:** Staff should be trained on the new security architecture, including how to use new tools and follow new procedures. Comprehensive documentation should be created to support ongoing operations and future updates.

Step 6: Monitor and Maintain the Architecture

Ongoing monitoring and maintenance are crucial to ensure that the architecture remains effective over time. This involves regularly reviewing security controls, conducting security assessments, and adjusting the architecture as necessary to respond to emerging threats.

- **Real-Time Monitoring:** Continuous monitoring of the security architecture is essential for detecting and responding to threats in real-time. This involves using tools like SIEM systems to collect and analyse security data across the organisation.
- **Routine Maintenance:** Security controls must be regularly maintained to ensure they remain effective. This includes applying patches and updates, reviewing access controls, and testing backup and recovery procedures.
- **Periodic Reviews:** Regular security reviews should be conducted to assess the effectiveness of the architecture and identify areas for improvement. These reviews should be based on both internal assessments and external audits.

Step 7: Review and Update the Architecture

As the organisation evolves and the threat landscape changes, the security architecture must be reviewed and updated. This iterative process ensures that the architecture continues to meet the organisation's needs and adapts to new challenges.

- **Evolving Threat Landscape:** The security environment is constantly changing, with new threats emerging and existing threats evolving. The architecture must be regularly updated to address these changes, incorporating new technologies and best practices as needed.
- **Adapting to Organisational Changes:** As the organisation grows or changes direction, its security needs may also change. The architecture must be flexible enough to adapt to these changes, whether that means scaling to support new users or integrating new technologies.
- **Continuous Improvement:** The architecture should be subject to continuous improvement, with lessons learned from incidents and assessments used to inform future updates. This proactive approach helps ensure that the architecture remains resilient and effective over time.

Tailoring Security Architectures to Different Environments

Different environments present unique security challenges, and the security architecture must be tailored accordingly. Whether designing for on-premises infrastructure, cloud environments, or hybrid models, it's essential to consider the specific risks and requirements of each environment.

On-Premises Environments

On-premises environments offer organisations full control over their security infrastructure. However, this control also requires significant resources for management and maintenance, as well as a deep understanding of the organisation's specific security needs.

- **Physical Security:** Physical security is a critical consideration in on-premises environments. Data centres and other critical facilities must be secured against physical threats, with access controls, surveillance systems, and environmental protections in place.
- **Legacy Systems:** Many organisations rely on legacy systems that may not support modern security controls. In such cases, additional layers of protection, such as network segmentation or application gateways, can be implemented to secure these systems.
- **Scalability and Maintenance:** On-premises architectures must be designed with scalability in mind, ensuring that they can grow alongside the organisation. Regular maintenance is also essential, as on-premises systems typically require more hands-on management than cloud-based solutions.

Cloud Environments

Cloud environments introduce unique security challenges, particularly related to data protection, access control, and shared responsibility between the organisation and the Cloud Service Provider (CSP).

- **Shared Responsibility Model:** In cloud environments, security is a shared responsibility between the CSP and the customer. It is crucial to clearly define and understand these responsibilities to ensure that all aspects of security are covered.

- **Data Encryption:** Protecting data in the cloud requires robust encryption for both data at rest and data in transit. Organisations must also ensure secure key management practices to prevent unauthorised access.
- **Access Control and Identity Management:** Cloud-based IAM solutions should enforce granular access controls, requiring multi-factor authentication and managing access to cloud resources based on roles and responsibilities. Ensuring that only authorised users have access to sensitive data is critical in cloud environments.
- **Compliance and Regulatory Considerations:** Ensuring compliance with regulations such as GDPR or HIPAA in the cloud requires careful management of data and security controls, especially when data is stored across multiple jurisdictions.

Hybrid Environments

Hybrid environments combine on-premises infrastructure with cloud services, requiring a cohesive security strategy that spans both environments.

- **Integration:** Security controls must be integrated across on-premises and cloud environments, providing consistent protection regardless of where data or applications reside. This requires careful coordination to ensure that security policies are applied uniformly across both environments.
- **Visibility:** Gaining visibility into both on-premises and cloud environments is crucial for effective security management. Tools like SIEM systems and Cloud Access Security Brokers (CASB) can provide centralised monitoring and management of security across hybrid environments.
- **Data Mobility:** Hybrid environments often involve the movement of data between on-premises and cloud systems. Security measures must protect data throughout its lifecycle, ensuring it remains secure during transit and storage.

Scaling Security Architectures

As organisations grow and evolve, their security architectures must scale to accommodate increased complexity, additional users, and expanded data volumes. Scaling involves not only expanding the architecture but also ensuring that security remains effective as the organisation grows.

Key Considerations for Scaling

- **Automation:** Automation plays a critical role in scaling security architectures. By automating routine security processes, such as patch management, threat detection, and incident response, organisations can reduce the need for manual intervention and improve efficiency.
- **Modular Design:** A modular approach to security architecture allows for components to be added, removed, or upgraded without disrupting the entire system. This flexibility is crucial for organisations that are rapidly expanding or that frequently integrate new technologies into their operations.
- **Cloud Services:** Cloud services offer on-demand scalability, enabling organisations to expand their security infrastructure without the need for significant capital investment. Cloud-based security solutions can quickly scale to meet increased demand, providing the flexibility needed to support growth.
- **Performance Monitoring:** Continuously monitoring the performance of security controls ensures they remain effective as the organisation grows. Regular reviews and adjustments are necessary to maintain optimal performance and address any new challenges that arise as the architecture scales.
- **Collaboration and Governance:** As security architectures scale, collaboration between security, IT, and business teams becomes increasingly important. Effective governance ensures that security considerations are integrated into all aspects of the organisation's growth strategy, aligning security with business objectives and ensuring that security scales in tandem with the organisation.

Conclusion

Designing a security architecture is a complex yet essential task that requires careful planning, collaboration, and a deep understanding of the organisation's needs and challenges. By adhering to the principles of security architecture design, conducting detailed risk assessments, and tailoring the architecture to different environments, organisations can build a robust, scalable security framework that protects their assets and supports their business objectives.

In the next chapter, we'll explore the implementation of security solutions, focusing on best practices for selecting, deploying, and managing security technologies. We'll also discuss how to balance security with operational efficiency, ensuring that your security investments deliver maximum value.

7
Implementing Security Solutions

Introduction to Implementing Security Solutions

Implementing security solutions is the critical phase, where strategic plans and designs come together into a functional and protective security infrastructure. This process is not just about installing software or configuring hardware; it's about integrating these solutions into the organisation's broader security architecture to create a cohesive and resilient defence mechanism. The effectiveness of this implementation lies in its ability to protect assets while supporting business operations seamlessly.

The implementation of security solutions requires a strategic approach, careful planning, and a deep understanding of the organisation's unique environment. It involves selecting the right technologies, deploying them effectively, and ensuring that they operate optimally over time. Moreover, it requires balancing robust security with operational efficiency to ensure that security measures do not impede the organisations productivity.

In this chapter, we will explore best practices for selecting, deploying, and managing security technologies. We will also discuss the challenges of balancing security with business needs, and how to ensure that your security investments deliver maximum value.

Selecting the Right Security Technologies

Choosing the appropriate security technologies is a critical first step in the implementation process. With the vast array of options available, selecting the right solution requires a thorough understanding of the organisation's specific security needs, existing infrastructure, and future growth plans.

DOI: 10.1201/9781003585923-7

Key Considerations for Technology Selection

1. Alignment with Security Requirements
    - **Understanding Needs:** The chosen technology must address the organisation's specific security needs, which are determined by the risk assessment and the overall security strategy. This alignment ensures that the solution effectively mitigates identified risks and supports the organisation's security goals.
    - **Tailored Solutions:** It's important to avoid one-size-fits-all solutions. Instead, focus on technologies that are tailored to meet the unique challenges of your environment. For example, a company with a high volume of sensitive customer data may prioritise encryption and Data Loss Prevention (DLP) technologies.
2. Integration with Existing Systems
    - **Seamless Integration:** The selected security technology must integrate seamlessly with the existing infrastructure. This includes ensuring compatibility with legacy systems, databases, and existing security protocols. Seamless integration reduces the risk of creating vulnerabilities and ensures that the new technology complements rather than disrupts the current system.
    - **API and Interoperability:** Consider technologies that offer robust APIs and support for interoperability, allowing for smoother integration with other systems and processes. This is especially critical in complex environments with multiple, interconnected systems.
3. Scalability
    - **Future-Proofing:** The security solution should be capable of scaling as the organisation grows. This means being able to handle an increasing number of users, expanding data volumes, and accommodating more complex infrastructures without compromising performance or security.
    - **Modular and Flexible Design:** Choose solutions that are modular and can be expanded or adjusted as needed. This approach allows for incremental upgrades and adjustments as the organisation's needs evolve.

4. User Experience
   - **Ease of Use:** Security technologies should be user-friendly and not overly complex. If the solution is difficult to use, it can lead to errors, workarounds, or resistance from users, which in turn can create security gaps.
   - **User Adoption:** High user adoption is critical for the success of security measures. Technologies that integrate smoothly into users' workflows without causing significant disruption are more likely to be embraced by the organisation.
5. Vendor Support and Reputation
   - **Reliable Support:** The quality of vendor support can significantly impact the success of a security solution. Vendors should offer robust support services, including timely updates, security patches, and responsive customer service.
   - **Proven Track Record:** Consider the vendor's reputation and track record in the industry. Solutions from established vendors with a history of strong performance and reliable service are generally safer bets.
6. Total Cost of Ownership (TCO)
   - **Long-Term Investment**: The cost of the technology should be considered in terms of TCO, which includes not only the initial purchase price but also ongoing costs such as maintenance, support, upgrades, and any necessary training.
   - **Value for Money:** It's important to ensure that the selected solution provides value for money. This means that the investment should contribute to reducing risks, enhancing security, and ultimately supporting the organisation's business objectives.

Best Practices for Deploying Security Solutions

Deployment is the phase where security technologies are integrated into the organisation's environment. This process must be executed meticulously to ensure that the solutions function as intended and enhance the overall security posture without introducing new vulnerabilities.

Key Steps in the Deployment Process

1. Develop a Detailed Deployment Plan
    - **Comprehensive Planning:** A detailed deployment plan is essential for successful implementation. This plan should outline every step of the deployment process, the resources required, the timeline, and the roles and responsibilities of all team members involved.
    - **Risk Mitigation:** The plan should include risk mitigation strategies to address potential issues that may arise during deployment. This includes contingency plans for delays, integration challenges, or unexpected technical issues.
2. Conduct a Pilot Test
    - **Controlled Environment Testing:** Before full-scale deployment, a pilot test should be conducted in a controlled environment. This allows the organisation to identify and resolve potential issues without affecting the entire operation.
    - **Performance Assessment:** During the pilot test, assess the solution's performance, usability, and compatibility with existing systems. This step is crucial for ensuring that the solution will function effectively when fully implemented.
3. Ensure Compatibility
    - **System Compatibility:** During deployment, it's vital to confirm that the new solution is compatible with existing systems and adheres to the organisation's security policies. This involves careful configuration and testing to prevent any disruptions or security lapses.
    - **Cross-functional Integration:** In complex environments, the new technology must work seamlessly across different departments and systems. Ensuring compatibility across the board is key to maintaining operational continuity.
4. Provide Comprehensive Training

- **Technical Training:** IT staff must be thoroughly trained on the technical aspects of managing the new security solution. This includes installation, configuration, troubleshooting, and regular maintenance.
- **User Training:** End-users should also receive training on how to interact with the new system, particularly if the solution involves changes to their regular workflows or introduces new security protocols.

5. Monitor the Deployment
   - **Real-Time Monitoring:** Continuous monitoring during the deployment phase helps identify and address any issues in real time. This proactive approach ensures that the implementation process runs smoothly and that the solution integrates effectively into the organisation's security framework.
   - **Feedback Loops:** Establish feedback loops with IT staff and end-users to gather insights on the deployment process. This feedback is valuable for making immediate adjustments and improving future deployment processes.
6. Conduct a Post-deployment Review
   - **Comprehensive Evaluation:** After full deployment, conduct a thorough review to assess whether the solution meets all security requirements and performs as expected. This review should include an evaluation of system performance, user experience, and alignment with business objectives.
   - **Continuous Improvement:** Use the insights gained from the post-deployment review to make any necessary adjustments and to inform future implementations. Continuous improvement is key to maintaining an effective security posture.

Managing Security Solutions over Time

Once implemented, security solutions require ongoing management to ensure they remain effective. This involves continuous monitoring, regular updates, and proactive management to adapt to new threats and evolving business needs.

Key Aspects of Ongoing Management

1. Monitoring and Reporting
    - **Continuous Vigilance:** Continuous monitoring of security solutions is crucial for detecting and responding to threats in real time. Effective monitoring involves setting up automated alerts for suspicious activities and generating regular reports on system performance and security incidents.
    - **Detailed Reporting:** Regular reporting on the performance and status of security solutions is essential for identifying trends, potential vulnerabilities, and areas that may require additional attention or resources.
2. Patching and Updates
    - **Regular Updates:** Keeping security solutions up to date is critical for protecting against new vulnerabilities. This includes applying patches, updating software to the latest versions, and ensuring that all configurations are current and secure.
    - **Automated Patch Management:** Consider implementing automated patch management solutions to streamline the update process and ensure that all systems are consistently protected.
3. Performance Optimisation
    - **Regular Assessments:** Over time, it's important to regularly assess and optimise the performance of security solutions. This may involve adjusting configurations, fine-tuning security policies, or upgrading hardware to improve efficiency.
    - **Resource Management:** Efficient resource management is key to maintaining optimal performance. This includes ensuring that security solutions are not overburdened and that they are capable of handling the organisation's demands.
4. Compliance Management
    - **Regulatory Alignment:** Security solutions must be managed in accordance with regulatory requirements and industry standards. This includes ensuring that security

configurations comply with relevant laws and conducting regular audits to verify compliance.

- **Documentation and Audits:** Maintain detailed documentation of all security measures and configurations. Regular audits should be conducted to ensure ongoing compliance and to identify any areas that may require adjustments.

5. Incident Response and Recovery
    - **Integrated Incident Response:** Security solutions should be integrated into the organisation's incident response plan. This ensures that the solutions can detect and respond to incidents in real time and that recovery procedures are in place to restore normal operations as quickly as possible.
    - **Preparedness Drills:** Conduct regular incident response drills to ensure that all systems and personnel are prepared to respond effectively to security incidents. These drills should be used to refine and improve response strategies.
6. Continuous Improvement
    - **Adaptation to New Threats:** Security is a dynamic field, and solutions must evolve to address new challenges. Regular reviews and updates are necessary to adapt to emerging threats and changing business needs.
    - **Innovation and Exploration:** Stay informed about new technologies and trends in security. Continuously explore opportunities to enhance the organisation's security posture through innovative solutions and approaches.

Balancing Security and Operational Efficiency

One of the key challenges in implementing security solutions is achieving a balance between robust security and operational efficiency. While it's essential to protect the organisation's assets, security measures should not hinder productivity or negatively impact the user experience.

Strategies for Balancing Security and Efficiency

1. Risk-Based Approach
   - **Focused Resource Allocation:** Prioritise security measures based on the level of risk, ensuring that resources are focused on protecting the most critical assets without overburdening the system with unnecessary controls.
   - **Targeted Security Investments:** Invest in security measures that address the most significant threats while avoiding over-investment in areas with lower risk. This approach ensures that resources are used effectively.
2. User-Centred Design
   - **Engaging Users in Design:** Involve end-users in the design and implementation of security solutions to ensure that the measures are user-friendly and do not create unnecessary barriers to productivity.
   - **Simplifying Security Processes:** Wherever possible, simplify security processes to make them easier for users to follow. This can help reduce errors and increase compliance with security protocols.
3. Automation
   - **Efficiency Through Automation:** Automate routine security tasks to reduce the burden on IT staff and improve efficiency. Automation can streamline processes such as patch management, threat detection, and incident response, allowing the security team to focus on more strategic activities.
   - **Scalability and Flexibility:** Automated solutions are often more scalable and flexible, making them ideal for organisations that are growing or that operate in dynamic environments.
4. Scalable Solutions
   - **Growth-Aligned Security:** Choose security solutions that can scale with the organisation's growth, ensuring that they can handle increased demands without requiring significant infrastructure changes.
   - **Modular Deployment:** Implement security solutions in a modular fashion, allowing for incremental upgrades and

adjustments as the organisation grows and its security needs evolve.

5. Regular Training and Awareness
    - **Empowering Employees:** Regularly train employees on security best practices and make them aware of their role in maintaining security. A well-informed workforce is a critical line of defence against security threats.
    - **Ongoing Education:** Security awareness should be an ongoing effort, with regular updates and refresher courses to keep employees informed about the latest threats and best practices.

Conclusion

Implementing security solutions is a critical phase in building a resilient security architecture that not only protects an organisation's assets but also supports its business objectives. By carefully selecting the right technologies, deploying them effectively, and managing them over time, organisations can ensure that their security measures provide robust protection while maintaining operational efficiency.

Balancing security with efficiency is essential for ensuring that security measures do not impede productivity or negatively impact the user experience. With thoughtful planning, collaboration, and a commitment to continuous improvement, organisations can ensure that their security investments deliver maximum value, enabling them to stay ahead in an increasingly complex and dynamic threat landscape.

The next chapter will explore advanced topics in enterprise security, including emerging threats, the role of artificial intelligence in security, and the implementation of Zero Trust architectures. These topics are essential for staying ahead of the curve in a rapidly evolving threat landscape.

8

Advanced Topics in Enterprise Security

Introduction to Advanced Security Concepts

Today, the cybersecurity landscape evolving at a rapid pace. Protecting organisational assets demands more than just foundational security measures that look at user endpoints or only defend the environments boundary. As technology advances and digital footprints expand, the complexities and challenges of safeguarding these assets grow exponentially. Advanced security topics are crucial for modern enterprises to stay ahead of emerging threats, adapt to new technologies, and implement cutting-edge strategies that enhance their overall security posture.

This chapter covers several advanced topics essential for maintaining a strong security stance, including emerging threats, the role of Artificial Intelligence (AI) in security, the implementation of Zero Trust architectures, and advanced encryption techniques. We'll also discuss the importance of threat intelligence, the challenges of securing Internet of Things (IoT) devices, the difficulties of implementing network segmentation, and the impact of regulatory changes on security practices. By mastering these advanced concepts, organisations can fortify their defences against sophisticated cyber threats and ensure long-term resilience.

Emerging Threats in Cybersecurity

The threat landscape in cybersecurity is constantly shifting as attackers develop new tactics, techniques, and procedures. Organisations must stay vigilant, continuously updating their strategies to address these evolving threats effectively.

DOI: 10.1201/9781003585923-8

Key Emerging Threats

- **Advanced Persistent Threats (APTs):** These are prolonged, targeted attacks where adversaries stealthily infiltrate an organisation's network, often aiming to steal sensitive information or disrupt operations over an extended period. APTs are typically carried out by well-funded and highly skilled actors, such as state-sponsored groups.
- **Ransomware:** Ransomware attacks have grown in sophistication, with attackers using complex encryption techniques to lock victims out of their systems until a ransom is paid. This type of malware can cause severe operational disruptions and significant financial losses.
- **Supply Chain Attacks:** By targeting third-party vendors, suppliers, or service providers, attackers can infiltrate an organisation's network through its trusted partners. This indirect approach makes supply chain attacks particularly insidious and challenging to detect.
- **Fileless Malware:** Unlike traditional malware, fileless malware operates in-memory, exploiting legitimate system processes without leaving a file trace. This stealthy nature makes it difficult to detect and mitigate using conventional antivirus solutions.
- **Deepfakes:** Deepfake technology leverages AI to create highly realistic but fake videos, audio, or images. These can be used in social engineering attacks, disinformation campaigns, or even financial fraud, where victims are deceived by fabricated content.
- **IoT Vulnerabilities:** The proliferation of IoT devices introduces new security risks, as many of these devices are inadequately secured and can be exploited as entry points into larger networks or enlisted into botnets for large-scale attacks.

Strategies for Addressing Emerging Threats

- **Threat Intelligence:** Developing robust threat intelligence capabilities allows organisations to stay ahead of emerging threats by gathering and analysing information on new attack vectors, tactics, and threat actors.

- **Advanced Detection and Response:** Deploying advanced detection and response tools, such as Endpoint Detection and Response (EDR) and Security Orchestration, Automation, and Response (SOAR), enables real-time threat detection and rapid response to mitigate potential impacts.
- **Regular Security Assessments:** Conducting regular penetration tests, vulnerability assessments, and red teaming exercises helps identify and address vulnerabilities before they can be exploited.
- **Supply Chain Security:** Enhancing supply chain security involves rigorous vetting of suppliers, enforcing security requirements in contracts, and continuously monitoring third-party interactions with the organisation's systems.

The Role of Artificial Intelligence in Security

Artificial Intelligence (AI) is revolutionising cybersecurity by enabling more sophisticated threat detection, prevention, and response capabilities. AI-driven security solutions can process vast amounts of data at high speed, identify subtle patterns indicative of malicious activity, and automate responses to potential threats.

Applications of AI in Security

- **Threat Detection and Analysis:** AI can process large datasets to detect anomalies and patterns associated with cyber threats. Machine learning algorithms improve over time, allowing for the identification of both known and novel threats.
- **Automated Incident Response:** AI can automate various aspects of incident response, such as isolating compromised systems, neutralising threats, and triggering alerts. This automation reduces response times and mitigates the impact of attacks.
- **Predictive Security:** AI can be used to predict potential threats by analysing historical data and identifying trends

that precede security incidents. This proactive approach helps in preventing attacks before they occur.

- **Fraud Detection:** In industries like finance, AI is instrumental in detecting fraudulent activities by analysing transaction patterns and identifying anomalies that could indicate fraudulent behaviour.
- **User Behaviour Analytics (UBA):** AI can monitor user behaviour to detect deviations from established patterns, which may signal insider threats or compromised accounts. UBA helps in identifying and responding to these threats in real time.

Challenges and Considerations

- **AI-Driven Attacks:** Just as AI enhances defensive capabilities; it can also be weaponised by attackers to create more sophisticated and adaptive threats. AI could be used to automate phishing campaigns, optimise malware, or conduct large-scale attacks with precision.
- **Bias and Ethics:** AI systems are susceptible to biases in the data they are trained on, which can lead to skewed outcomes. In cybersecurity, biased AI could result in incorrect threat assessments or discriminatory practices.
- **Transparency and Accountability:** AI's decision-making processes can be opaque, making it difficult to understand or justify certain actions. This lack of transparency can pose challenges in compliance, auditing, and accountability.
- **Integration with Human Expertise:** While AI is a powerful tool, it should complement rather than replace human expertise. Security professionals are crucial in interpreting AI outputs, making strategic decisions, and managing the ethical implications of AI in security.

Implementing Zero Trust Architectures

Zero Trust is a security framework that assumes no user or device should be trusted by default, even if they are inside the network.

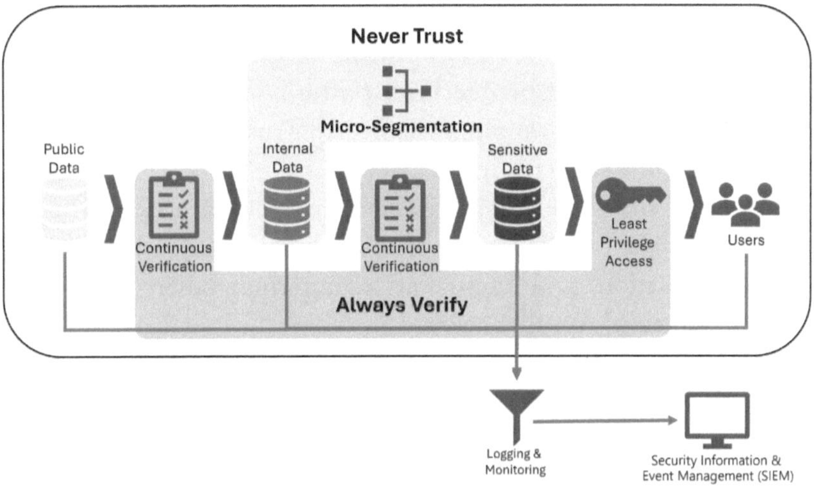

Figure 8.1 Zero Trust architecture: segmented network with continuous verification and least privilege access.

Instead, every access request is treated as potentially malicious and is subject to stringent verification processes (Figure 8.1). Implementing Zero Trust architectures helps organisations reduce the risk of data breaches by enforcing strict access controls and continuously monitoring all network activity.

Core Principles of Zero Trust

1. **Verify Explicitly:** Always authenticate and authorise users, devices, and applications before granting access. This involves multi-factor authentication, device compliance checks, and continuous monitoring.
2. **Limit Access with Least Privilege:** Restrict access rights to the minimum necessary for users and devices to perform their tasks. Access should be regularly reviewed and adjusted to reflect changes in roles or risk profiles.
3. **Assume Breach:** Operate under the assumption that a breach has already occurred or is imminent. This mindset drives the implementation of segmentation, monitoring, and quick response measures to limit damage.

Steps to Implement Zero Trust

1. **Assess the Current Environment:** Begin by evaluating the organisation's existing security posture, identifying vulnerabilities, and determining where Zero Trust principles can be applied most effectively.
2. **Design the Zero Trust Architecture:** Develop a Zero Trust model that incorporates multi-factor authentication, micro-segmentation, and continuous monitoring, tailored to the organisation's specific needs.
3. **Implement Identity and Access Management (IAM):** Deploy IAM solutions that enforce stringent access controls based on the principle of least privilege and continuously verify the identity of users and devices.
4. **Deploy Network Segmentation and Micro-segmentation:** Segment the network into isolated zones to prevent lateral movement by attackers. Micro-segmentation further divides these zones to enforce granular access controls.
5. **Implement Continuous Monitoring and Analytics:** Use real-time monitoring tools to detect anomalies and potential breaches as they occur. Analytics can help identify suspicious patterns and automate responses to threats.
6. **Automate Threat Detection and Response:** Leverage automation tools like EDR and SOAR to detect threats quickly and respond effectively, reducing the window of opportunity for attackers.
7. **Regularly Review and Update the Architecture:** Zero Trust requires ongoing assessment and refinement to remain effective. Regularly updating the architecture ensures it can adapt to new threats and organisational changes.

Challenges in Implementing Network Segmentation

- **Complexity:** Network segmentation, particularly micro-segmentation, introduces complexity into the network infrastructure. Managing multiple isolated zones and ensuring they function seamlessly requires advanced planning and coordination.
- **Performance Impact:** Segmentation can impact network performance, especially if not implemented with performance

considerations in mind. Increased latency, network congestion, or difficulties in managing data flow between zones can arise if segmentation is not carefully planned.

- **Integration with Legacy Systems:** Older systems and applications may not be designed with segmentation in mind, making it difficult to integrate them into a segmented network. Retrofitting these systems can be resource-intensive and may introduce new vulnerabilities if not done correctly.
- **Ongoing Management:** Once implemented, segmented networks require continuous management to ensure that access controls remain effective, configurations are up to date, and performance issues are addressed promptly.
- **User Resistance:** Segmentation often requires changes to user workflows, such as more frequent authentication checks or restricted access to certain resources. Without proper training and communication, users may resist these changes or find ways to bypass security measures.

Advanced Encryption Techniques

As cyber threats become more sophisticated, encryption techniques must also evolve to ensure data remains secure. Advanced encryption techniques enhance traditional methods, offering stronger protection against emerging threats and addressing specific security needs in modern IT environments (Figure 8.2).

Key Advanced Encryption Techniques

1. **Quantum-Resistant Encryption:** With the advent of quantum computing, traditional encryption algorithms such as RSA and ECC are at risk of being broken. Quantum-resistant encryption, also known as post-quantum cryptography, is being developed to safeguard data against future quantum attacks.
2. **Homomorphic Encryption:** This allows computations to be performed on encrypted data without needing to decrypt it first. Homomorphic encryption enables secure data processing in untrusted environments, such as cloud computing, without exposing sensitive information.

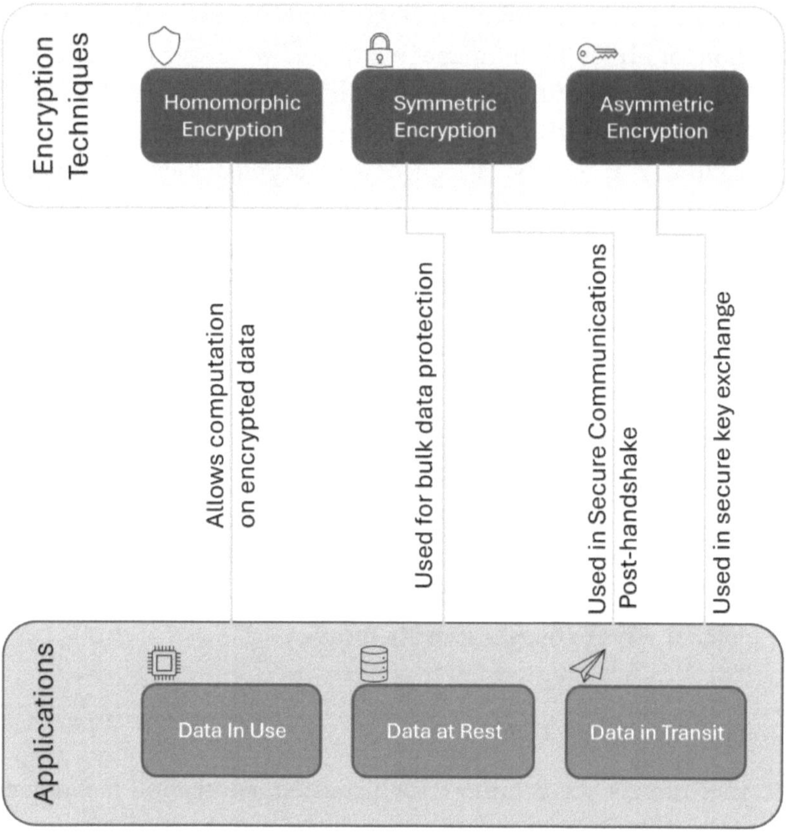

Figure 8.2 Encryption techniques and their applications. This diagram shows how encryption is used to protect data at rest, in transit, and in use.

3. **Blockchain-Based Encryption:** Blockchain technology can be leveraged for secure key management and data integrity verification, enhancing traditional encryption methods with decentralised and tamper-resistant features.
4. **Multi-Party Computation (MPC):** MPC allows multiple parties to jointly compute a function over their inputs while keeping those inputs private. This technique is valuable for collaborative environments where data privacy must be maintained.
5. **Attribute-Based Encryption (ABE):** ABE enables encryption and decryption based on specific attributes, such as user roles or access policies. This allows for more granular access control and is particularly useful in complex organisational environments.

Implementing Advanced Encryption Techniques

- **Assess Encryption Needs:** Begin by evaluating the organisation's specific encryption requirements, considering factors like data sensitivity, regulatory obligations, and potential future threats.
- **Evaluate and Select Encryption Algorithms:** Choose the most appropriate advanced encryption techniques based on security needs, performance considerations, and compatibility with existing systems.
- **Implement Encryption Management Solutions:** Deploy tools and processes for the secure generation, storage, and distribution of encryption keys, ensuring that encryption practices remain robust and scalable.
- **Monitor and Update Encryption Practices:** Regularly review and enhance encryption practices to keep pace with technological advancements and emerging threats, ensuring long-term data security.

Conclusion

Advanced topics in enterprise security, such as emerging threats, AI-driven security, Zero Trust architectures, and advanced encryption techniques, are crucial for organisations seeking to maintain a robust security posture in a rapidly evolving threat landscape. By understanding and implementing these advanced concepts, organisations can better protect their assets, respond to sophisticated attacks, and ensure resilience in the face of new challenges.

In the next chapter, we'll explore the future of enterprise security, focusing on trends and innovations that are shaping the next generation of cybersecurity solutions. We'll also discuss how organisations can prepare for the challenges and opportunities that lie ahead.

9
Case Studies

Introduction to Case Studies

Case studies provide invaluable insights into how organisations have successfully implemented security architectures and solutions to tackle their unique challenges. In this chapter, we explore a series of real-world use cases that illustrate the practical application of enterprise security practices across different industries. However, to protect the confidentiality of the organisations involved, these case studies have been normalised and sanitised. This means that while the scenarios, challenges, and solutions presented are drawn from actual events, certain details have been modified to ensure privacy and confidentiality.

These case studies highlight the importance of tailoring security solutions to meet specific organisational needs, the hurdles encountered during implementation, and the lessons learned from each experience. By examining these examples, we gain a deeper understanding of how various sectors, ranging from finance and healthcare to technology and retail, approach security. Additionally, we discuss the broader industry implications of these cases, providing a comprehensive view of how modern enterprises are adapting to an ever-evolving cybersecurity landscape.

Case Study 1: Financial Institution Implementing a Zero Trust Architecture

Overview

A large financial institution, operating across multiple countries, faced a surge in cybersecurity threats, including sophisticated phishing attacks, insider threats, and data breaches. The institution's security architecture, previously built around a traditional perimeter defence

DOI: 10.1201/9781003585923-9

model, was increasingly inadequate to safeguard its critical assets and meet the stringent regulatory demands of global financial services.

Challenges

- **Legacy Systems:** The institution's reliance on a mix of legacy systems and modern applications posed significant challenges in implementing consistent security controls across its network.
- **Distributed Workforce:** With a workforce spread across multiple locations, including remote offices, the institution needed a security model that could robustly protect its assets regardless of user location.
- **Regulatory Compliance:** The institution had to comply with strict regulatory requirements, including GDPR, PCI DSS, and various national banking regulations. Ensuring compliance across its global operations was a complex task.

Solutions Implemented

1. **Identity and Access Management (IAM):** A comprehensive IAM solution was implemented, featuring Multi-factor Authentication (MFA), Single Sign-On (SSO), and Role-Based Access Control (RBAC). These measures ensured that only authorised users could access sensitive systems, providing a significant boost to security across the institution's distributed workforce.
2. **Network Segmentation:** The institution introduced network segmentation and micro-segmentation to prevent lateral movement by potential attackers. The network was divided into isolated zones, each with tailored access controls to ensure that any breach would be contained within a specific segment.
3. **Continuous Monitoring and Threat Detection:** A Security Information and Event Management (SIEM) system, integrated with Endpoint Detection and Response (EDR) tools, was deployed to monitor network activity in real-time,

enabling the detection and mitigation of threats before they could escalate.

4. **Automated Incident Response:** The institution implemented a Security Orchestration, Automation, and Response (SOAR) platform to automate incident response processes, enabling faster and more effective responses to security incidents.

Outcomes

- **Enhanced Security Posture:** The adoption of a Zero Trust architecture led to a measurable reduction in security incidents, with a reported 40% decrease in successful phishing attacks and a significant drop in unauthorised access attempts. This bolstered the institution's overall security posture.
- **Improved Compliance:** The new security architecture ensured full compliance with GDPR, PCI DSS, and other applicable regulations. Regular audits showed a 95% compliance rate, with only minor adjustments needed, greatly reducing the risk of regulatory fines.
- **Operational Efficiency:** The SOAR platform improved response times to security incidents by 50%, freeing up the security team to focus on more strategic tasks. The automation of routine tasks also reduced the workload by 30%, leading to significant time and cost savings.

Broader Industry Implications

This case underscores the growing importance of Zero Trust architectures in the financial sector, particularly as organisations deal with increasingly sophisticated cyber threats and complex regulatory environments. The shift from traditional perimeter defences to Zero Trust models reflects a broader trend within the industry towards more adaptive and resilient security frameworks. As financial institutions continue to face evolving threats, the lessons learned from this case study highlight the necessity of integrating advanced IAM solutions and automated incident response capabilities to maintain robust security postures.

Case Study 2: Healthcare Organisation Securing Patient Data in the Cloud

Overview

A large healthcare organisation embarked on a project to migrate its Electronic Health Record (EHR) system to the cloud to benefit from scalability, cost savings, and improved accessibility. However, this transition introduced significant security challenges, particularly in protecting sensitive patient data while maintaining compliance with stringent healthcare regulations like HIPAA.

Challenges

- **Data Protection:** Ensuring the security of patient data, both at rest and in transit, was a critical concern to prevent unauthorised access or breaches.
- **Access Control:** The organisation needed robust access controls to manage healthcare providers accessing the EHR system from various locations, including hospitals, clinics, and remote sites.
- **Regulatory Compliance:** Compliance with HIPAA and other healthcare regulations was mandatory, requiring strict security controls to avoid legal penalties and protect the organisation's reputation.

Solutions Implemented

1. **Cloud Identity and Access Management (IAM):** A cloud-based IAM solution was deployed to enforce MFA, RBAC, and SSO, ensuring that only authorised healthcare providers could access patient data.
2. **Data Encryption:** The organisation implemented end-to-end encryption for both data at rest and in transit, supported by a dedicated Key Management Service (KMS) to securely manage encryption keys.
3. **Continuous Monitoring and Compliance Auditing:** A Cloud Security Posture Management (CSPM) solution was deployed to continuously monitor the cloud environment for

security risks and ensure compliance with HIPAA requirements through automated auditing.

4. **Data Loss Prevention (DLP):** A cloud-based DLP solution was integrated to monitor and control the flow of sensitive information, preventing unauthorised sharing or leakage of patient data.

Outcomes

- **Enhanced Data Security:** The deployment of encryption, IAM, and DLP solutions resulted in a 60% reduction in security incidents involving unauthorised access to patient data. No significant data breaches were reported post-implementation, marking a major improvement in data protection.
- **HIPAA Compliance:** The CSPM solution helped the organisation achieve a 98% compliance rate with HIPAA requirements, as confirmed by external audits, reducing the risk of regulatory penalties and enhancing the organisation's reputation.
- **Scalability and Efficiency:** The cloud-based security solutions provided the flexibility to scale the EHR system seamlessly, accommodating a 30% increase in patient data without compromising security. Operational efficiency improved by 25%, with automated compliance audits freeing up resources for other critical tasks.

Broader Industry Implications

This case illustrates the increasing reliance on cloud solutions in the healthcare sector and the accompanying need for robust security frameworks that ensure compliance and data protection. As more healthcare organisations migrate to the cloud, the lessons learned here emphasise the importance of integrating cloud-specific security measures such as IAM, encryption, and continuous compliance monitoring. The success of this implementation highlights the potential for cloud solutions to enhance both security and operational efficiency in the healthcare industry, paving the way for broader adoption.

Case Study 3: Technology Company Mitigating Insider Threats

Overview

A mid-sized technology company faced a growing number of insider threats, including data leaks and unauthorised access to sensitive information. The company's existing security measures were primarily focused on external threats, leaving it vulnerable to attacks from within. To address this issue, the company implemented a comprehensive insider threat mitigation strategy, combining technological solutions with organisational measures.

Challenges

- **Data Leakage:** Previous incidents involving the leakage of sensitive information had led to significant financial losses and damage to the company's reputation.
- **Unauthorised Access:** Instances of employees gaining unauthorised access to systems and data beyond their job responsibilities raised concerns about privilege creep and potential abuse of access rights.
- **Employee Awareness:** There was a general lack of awareness among employees about the risks associated with their actions, such as sharing sensitive information through unsecured channels.

Solutions Implemented

1. **User Behaviour Analytics (UBA):** The company implemented UBA to monitor employee activity and detect anomalies that could indicate insider threats, establishing a baseline of normal behaviour to flag deviations.
2. **Data Loss Prevention (DLP):** A DLP solution was deployed to monitor and control the flow of sensitive information, enforcing policies to prevent unauthorised sharing both internally and externally.
3. **Access Control and Privilege Management:** The company enforced stricter access control policies, including RBAC and

Privileged Access Management (PAM), to minimise the risk of privilege abuse and ensure employees had access only to the systems necessary for their roles.

4. **Security Awareness Training:** A comprehensive security awareness training program was launched to educate employees on the risks of insider threats and the importance of adhering to security policies.

Outcomes

- **Reduced Insider Threats:** The UBA and DLP solutions led to a 50% reduction in incidents of unauthorised access and data leakage within the first year of implementation, significantly mitigating the risk of insider threats.
- **Improved Security Culture:** Security awareness training resulted in a 40% increase in the reporting of suspicious activities by employees, indicating a stronger security culture within the organisation.
- **Enhanced Access Control:** The enforcement of RBAC and PAM policies reduced privilege creep by 60%, ensuring that access to sensitive data was tightly controlled and monitored.

Broader Industry Implications

The growing threat of insider attacks across industries underscores the importance of proactive measures like UBA and DLP. As organisations become more complex and employees have access to increasingly sensitive information, the need for robust insider threat mitigation strategies becomes critical. This case study highlights the effectiveness of combining technological solutions with organisational changes, such as security awareness training, to create a comprehensive defence against insider threats. The success of this approach suggests that similar strategies could be beneficial across a wide range of sectors, particularly those handling highly sensitive data.

Case Study 4: Retailer Protecting Customer Data and Payment Systems

Overview

A large retail chain with both physical and online stores faced escalating cybersecurity threats, particularly targeting its customer data and payment systems. Following several data breaches that resulted in financial losses and reputational damage, the retailer decided to overhaul its security architecture to better protect its critical assets.

Challenges

- **Customer Data Protection:** The retailer needed to secure vast amounts of customer data, including Personally Identifiable Information (PII) and Payment Card Information (PCI), to maintain customer trust and comply with data protection regulations.
- **Payment System Security:** Protecting payment systems from cybercriminals seeking to steal card information and carry out fraudulent transactions was a top priority.
- **Compliance Requirements:** The retailer had to meet various regulatory requirements, including PCI DSS and GDPR, necessitating robust security controls to avoid penalties and safeguard its reputation.

Solutions Implemented

1. **Data Encryption:** End-to-end encryption was implemented for customer data, ensuring it was protected both at rest and in transit. Encryption keys were managed securely to prevent unauthorised access.
2. **Tokenisation:** To protect payment card information, tokenisation was introduced, replacing sensitive card data with tokens that could not be used outside the retailer's systems.
3. **Network Segmentation:** The retailer segmented its network to isolate payment systems and customer data from other parts of the network, reducing the attack surface and preventing lateral movement by attackers.

4. **Compliance Management:** A compliance management solution was deployed to ensure adherence to PCI DSS and GDPR requirements through automated auditing, monitoring, and reporting.
5. **Incident Response and Recovery:** A comprehensive incident response and recovery plan was developed to quickly detect, respond to, and recover from security incidents, minimising the impact on operations.

Outcomes

- **Enhanced Data Security:** The introduction of encryption, tokenisation, and network segmentation resulted in a 70% reduction in security incidents involving customer data and payment systems. The retailer reported no significant breaches in the year following implementation.
- **Improved Compliance:** Automated compliance management enabled the retailer to maintain a 99% compliance rate with PCI DSS and GDPR, reducing the risk of regulatory fines and enhancing customer trust.
- **Resilience and Preparedness:** The incident response plan improved the retailer's ability to respond to security incidents, reducing response times by 40% and ensuring that critical operations could be quickly restored after an incident.

Broader Industry Implications

As cyber threats targeting the retail sector continue to evolve, the need for comprehensive security measures to protect customer data and payment systems becomes increasingly urgent. This case study illustrates the critical role that encryption, tokenisation, and network segmentation play in safeguarding sensitive information in the retail environment. The success of the retailer's approach demonstrates that similar strategies could be adopted by other organisations facing similar challenges, particularly as compliance requirements become more stringent and customer expectations for data security rise.

Conclusion

These enhanced case studies provide deeper insights into the practical application of enterprise security strategies across various industries. By examining these real-world examples, readers can better understand how organisations address unique security challenges, implement effective solutions, and achieve significant improvements in their security posture. The lessons learned and broader industry implications discussed in these cases offer valuable guidance for other organisations seeking to strengthen their defences in an increasingly complex threat landscape.

In the final chapter, we'll explore the future of enterprise security, focusing on emerging trends, technologies, and challenges that will shape the next generation of cybersecurity solutions. We'll discuss how organisations can prepare for the future and stay ahead of the evolving threat landscape.

10
Bridging Strategy and Practice

Reflecting on the Journey

As we conclude our deep dive into Enterprise Security Architecture (ESA), it's important to pause and reflect on the ground we've covered. Our exploration has been about much more than just understanding the mechanics of cybersecurity; it's been about embracing a fundamental shift in how security is perceived and implemented within modern organisations.

Throughout the previous chapters, we've touched on the complex landscape of enterprise security. We began by defining the foundational concepts, accepting that a well-defined security architecture is not just a technical blueprint but the backbone of an organisation's security posture. We saw how Governance, Risk Management, and Compliance (GRC) are not only regulatory checkboxes but strategic enablers that align security efforts with the wider business objectives.

We moved on to break down the critical components of Identity and Access Management (IAM), recognising its pivotal role in ensuring that the right people have the right access at the right times. IAM is about more than just preventing unauthorised access; it's about embedding accountability and traceability into every interaction within your digital ecosystem.

We highlighted network security as a frontline defence, protecting the infrastructure that underpins your organisations digital operations. Through our discussions on firewalls, Intrusion Detection Systems (IDS), and network segmentation, we built a layered defence strategy that is resilient to sophisticated threats. The introduction of the Zero Trust model underpinned the necessity to continually verify

DOI: 10.1201/9781003585923-10

trust within your systems, a practice that has become crucial in today's threat environment.

As we went further, we focused on securing the core assets of any organisation, applications and data. We explored secure software development principles, the importance of rigorous testing, and the necessity of data encryption in safeguarding sensitive information. In a world where data breaches can devastate an organisation, these practices are not optional, they are essential.

The rise of cloud computing added another layer of complexity, presenting both challenges and opportunities. We discussed the unique security considerations of the cloud, emphasising the shared responsibility model where cloud providers secure the infrastructure, but organisations remain responsible for their data and applications.

Our journey through advanced security technologies showcased how Artificial Intelligence (AI), machine learning, and automation are revolutionising cybersecurity. These tools are not just enhancing our ability to detect and respond to threats; they are transforming the very nature of security operations, making them more proactive, adaptive, and intelligent.

Yet, amidst all this technological advancement, we never lost sight of the human element.

> *The best security technology in the world is only as effective as the people who use it.*

We've repeatedly emphasised the importance of cultivating a security-aware culture, where every employee understands their role in protecting the organisation and is equipped to act responsibly.

Looking Forward: From Strategy to Action

As we transition from discussing the broad, strategic elements of Enterprise Security Architecture to more focused, tactical topics, it's clear that our work is just beginning. The principles and frameworks we've discussed are the foundation, but the true test lies in how effectively these strategies are implemented and adapted to meet the unique challenges of your organisation.

In the chapters ahead, our focus will shift towards operationalising these strategies. We'll explore how to build and manage a Security Operations Centre (SOC), the nerve centre of your security operations. A well-designed SOC is essential for real-time monitoring and rapid response to security incidents, ensuring that your organisation is always ready to defend against evolving threats.

Understanding that no system is impervious to attack, we'll also delve into the intricacies of incident response. Preparing for and managing security incidents effectively can mean the difference between a minor disruption and a major catastrophe. We'll guide you in developing an incident response plan that is both robust and flexible, capable of adapting to different scenarios.

Increasingly, automation and orchestration are becoming indispensable. We'll examine how these tools can streamline your security operations, allowing your team to focus on strategic initiatives rather than getting bogged down in routine tasks. Automation is not just about efficiency; it's about staying ahead of the curve in a fast-paced threat environment.

But security isn't just about technology and processes, it's about people. We'll explore strategies for building a security-first culture within your organisation, ensuring that security awareness permeates every level, from the C-suite to the front lines. This cultural shift is crucial for fostering an environment where security is everyone's responsibility.

As we move forward, we'll also consider the evolving landscape of cybersecurity careers. Whether you're building a security team or navigating your own career path, understanding the skills and competencies that are in demand will be crucial. We'll offer insights on how to prepare for the future, ensuring that both your organisation and you, personally, are equipped to meet the challenges ahead.

The future of cybersecurity is as dynamic as it is uncertain. New threats and trends are constantly emerging, and staying ahead requires not only vigilance but also innovation. We'll explore these developments, providing strategies to help you anticipate changes and fortify your defences.

Finally, our journey will culminate in the development of a holistic cybersecurity strategy that ties everything together. This strategy will integrate governance, risk management, advanced technologies, and human factors into a cohesive plan that aligns with your organisation's goals and adapts to an ever-changing threat landscape.

Key Takeaways

1. **Enterprise Security Architecture (ESA) as a Strategic Imperative:** ESA is not just a technical framework, it's a strategic asset that underpins your organisation's success. A well-designed ESA aligns security measures with business objectives, embedding security into every aspect of your operations.
2. **Strong Governance, Risk Management, and Compliance (GRC):** A robust GRC framework is essential for structured, consistent security practices that meet both internal and external standards. GRC creates a security culture that permeates every level of the organisation, ensuring long-term resilience.
3. **Identity and Access Management (IAM) Is Critical:** Controlling access to systems and data is fundamental to security. Implementing robust IAM solutions, including multi-factor authentication and role-based access control, protects sensitive information and streamlines compliance efforts.
4. **Network Security as the First Line of Defence:** Securing your network is paramount. By deploying layered defences such as firewalls, IDS/IPS, and network segmentation, and adopting a Zero Trust model, you create a resilient barrier against external threats.
5. **Application and Data Security:** Protecting data is more critical than ever. Secure development practices, data encryption, and data loss prevention solutions are vital for safeguarding sensitive information and mitigating the risk of data breaches.
6. **Cloud Security as a Priority:** Cloud environments present unique security challenges. By integrating cloud-specific security measures into your overall strategy, including encryption, identity management, and continuous monitoring, you can protect your data and applications effectively.
7. **Leveraging Advanced Security Technologies:** Embracing technologies like SIEM, EDR, and AI enhances threat

detection and response capabilities, allowing your organisation to stay ahead of emerging threats and respond with agility.

Final Thoughts: From Vision to Reality

As we transition into the next phase of our journey, remember that the strategies and frameworks we've discussed are just the beginning. The real challenge lies in translating these strategies into action, building systems that are not only secure but also adaptive and resilient in the face of change.

The chapters ahead will guide you through this process, providing detailed insights into the specific areas that are critical for maintaining a strong security posture. Together, we'll explore the operational, cultural, and technological dimensions of cybersecurity, ensuring that you're well-equipped to protect your organisation in today's complex digital landscape.

As we move forward, keep in mind that cybersecurity is not just about defending against threats, it's about enabling your organisation to thrive. By embedding security at the core of your operations, you're laying the groundwork for innovation, growth, and long-term success.

Our journey continues, and the best is yet to come!

11

Governance, Risk, and Compliance

Introduction to Governance, Risk, and Compliance (GRC)

Governance, Risk, and Compliance (GRC) forms the backbone of a comprehensive enterprise security strategy. In today's increasingly regulated and risk-prone business environment, GRC is essential not just for ensuring compliance with laws and regulations but for driving effective decision-making and aligning security with overall business objectives. A well-structured GRC framework enables organisations to navigate complex regulatory landscapes, manage risks proactively, and operate efficiently and ethically.

GRC is more than a set of guidelines or practices; it's a dynamic system that integrates governance structures, risk management processes, and compliance mechanisms into the fabric of the organisation. This integration ensures that security considerations are embedded into every aspect of business operations, fostering a culture of responsibility and vigilance.

In this chapter, we'll explore the essential components of a GRC framework, the steps involved in its implementation, and how it can be integrated into the broader enterprise security architecture (Figure 11.1). We'll also discuss the benefits that a strong GRC approach can bring to your organisation, such as enhanced decision-making, improved risk management, and strengthened regulatory compliance.

Understanding the Components of GRC

Governance: Setting the Foundation

Governance is the cornerstone of the GRC framework, providing the structure within which the organisation operates. It encompasses the

DOI: 10.1201/9781003585923-11

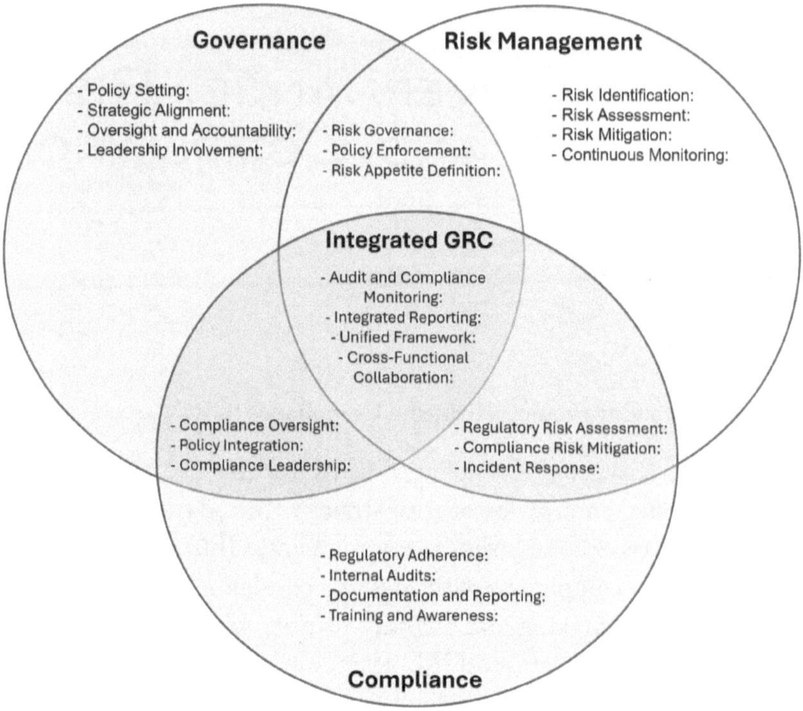

Figure 11.1 Venn diagram showing the integration of governance, risk management, and compliance, highlighting the key activities and their intersections within a unified GRC framework.

policies, procedures, and oversight mechanisms that ensure the organisation's activities align with its strategic goals and regulatory requirements. Governance involves not only the establishment of rules and guidelines but also the enforcement of these standards across all levels of the organisation.

Effective governance begins with strong leadership. Senior management and the board of directors must take an active role in setting the strategic direction for the organisation's security posture. This involves allocating resources appropriately, prioritising security initiatives that align with business objectives, and establishing accountability at all levels. Leadership must also foster a culture of transparency and ethical behaviour, where security is not seen as an obstacle but as an enabler of business success.

Policies and procedures are the tangible outputs of governance. They provide the roadmap for employees to follow, ensuring consistency in how security is managed across the organisation. These documents should cover a wide range of areas, including data protection, incident response, access controls, and third-party management. Importantly, policies should be living documents that evolve with the organisation and the external environment, regularly reviewed and updated to remain relevant.

Performance monitoring is another critical aspect of governance. Organisations must establish mechanisms to regularly assess the effectiveness of their governance practices. This includes conducting audits, tracking Key Performance Indicators (KPIs), and ensuring continuous improvement. Regular reporting to the board and senior management helps maintain visibility and ensures that governance remains aligned with the organisation's strategic goals.

Risk Management: Identifying and Mitigating Threats

Risk management is the proactive process of identifying, assessing, and mitigating risks that could negatively impact the organisation. In the context of GRC, risk management is not just about avoiding losses but about enabling the organisation to take calculated risks that drive growth and innovation. By understanding and managing risks, organisations can make informed decisions that balance opportunity with security.

The risk management process begins with risk identification. This involves a comprehensive assessment of both internal and external risks, ranging from cyber threats and data breaches to operational disruptions and regulatory changes. Organisations must look beyond immediate threats and consider long-term risks, such as the potential impact of new technologies or geopolitical shifts. Risk identification should be an ongoing activity, with regular updates to capture emerging risks.

Once risks are identified, they must be assessed to determine their likelihood and potential impact. This step is crucial for prioritising risks and ensuring that resources are allocated effectively. Risk assessment involves evaluating the severity of each risk, considering both quantitative and qualitative factors. This process should be informed by data, historical trends, and expert judgment.

After assessing risks, the next step is risk mitigation. This involves implementing strategies to reduce or eliminate the risks identified.

Mitigation strategies can include technical controls, such as firewalls and encryption, as well as organisational measures, like employee training and incident response planning. Risk mitigation is not a one-time effort but requires continuous monitoring and adjustment to adapt to new threats and changing business conditions.

Risk monitoring is essential to ensure that risk management strategies remain effective over time. Organisations must establish processes for tracking risks and their mitigation efforts, using tools such as risk registers and dashboards. Regular reviews and updates to the risk management process help maintain its relevance and effectiveness in a dynamic environment.

Compliance: Meeting Regulatory Requirements

Compliance is the process of adhering to laws, regulations, standards, and internal policies that govern the organisation's operations. In today's regulatory environment, compliance is more than just a legal obligation; it's a key factor in building and maintaining trust with customers, partners, and regulators. A strong compliance programme ensures that the organisation operates within the boundaries of the law while also aligning with industry best practices.

Regulatory awareness is the foundation of compliance. Organisations must stay informed about the regulations that apply to their industry and geographic locations. This includes understanding the specific requirements of laws such as the General Data Protection Regulation (GDPR), the Health Insurance Portability and Accountability Act (HIPAA), the Payment Card Industry Data Security Standard (PCI DSS), and others. Regulatory landscapes are constantly evolving, and organisations must be agile in adapting to new requirements.

Policy implementation is the practical aspect of compliance. It involves translating regulatory requirements into actionable policies and procedures that guide day-to-day operations. This includes implementing data protection measures, establishing access controls, and developing incident response plans. Effective policy implementation requires clear communication, adequate training, and robust enforcement mechanisms to ensure that all employees understand and adhere to compliance requirements.

Auditing and reporting are critical for demonstrating compliance. Regular audits, both internal and external, help verify that the organisation is adhering to its policies and regulatory requirements. Audits also provide valuable feedback on the effectiveness of the compliance programme, highlighting areas for improvement. Reporting, whether to regulators, stakeholders, or internally, ensures transparency and accountability.

Continuous improvement is essential in compliance. As regulations change and new risks emerge, organisations must regularly review and update their compliance programmes. This involves not only revising policies and procedures but also enhancing training programmes, adopting new technologies, and refining monitoring and reporting processes.

Implementing a GRC Framework

Implementing a GRC framework is a comprehensive process that requires careful planning, coordination, and integration across the organisation. It's not just about creating policies and procedures but about embedding GRC into the organisational culture and daily operations.

Steps to Implement a GRC Framework

1. **Define GRC Objectives:** Start by clearly defining what you want to achieve with your GRC programme. These objectives should be aligned with your business goals and tailored to your organisation's specific needs and risks. This will provide a clear direction for your GRC efforts and help prioritise resources effectively.
2. **Establish Leadership and Governance:** Governance begins with leadership. Establish a GRC committee or team that includes representatives from key departments such as IT, legal, finance, and operations. This team should be responsible for overseeing the GRC programme, setting strategic priorities, and ensuring alignment with overall business objectives.
3. **Develop Policies and Procedures:** Create comprehensive policies that cover all aspects of governance, risk management, and compliance. These policies should be detailed

enough to provide clear guidance but flexible enough to adapt to changing circumstances. Procedures should be developed to support these policies, ensuring that they are implemented consistently across the organisation.

4. **Implement Risk Management Processes:** Integrate risk management into your organisation's daily operations. Conduct regular risk assessments to identify potential threats, assess their impact, and prioritise mitigation efforts. Develop and implement mitigation strategies, and ensure that risks are continuously monitored and reviewed.
5. **Ensure Compliance with Regulations:** Build a compliance programme that addresses all relevant regulatory requirements. This includes implementing the necessary security controls, conducting regular audits, and providing ongoing training for employees. Ensure that your compliance programme is dynamic and capable of adapting to new regulations as they arise.
6. **Monitor and Review:** Continuous monitoring and regular review are essential for maintaining the effectiveness of your GRC programme. Use KPIs, dashboards, and regular audits to track progress, identify gaps, and make necessary adjustments. Regularly review and update your GRC framework to ensure it remains aligned with business goals and responsive to emerging threats and regulatory changes.

The Benefits of a Strong GRC Framework

A robust GRC framework provides numerous benefits that extend beyond just meeting regulatory requirements. It supports better decision-making, enhances risk management, and fosters a culture of accountability and continuous improvement. By integrating GRC into the core of your operations, you not only protect your organisation from potential threats but also position it for long-term success.

1. **Improved Decision-Making:** With a structured approach to governance, risk management, and compliance, your organisation can make more informed decisions that align with its strategic objectives. This leads to better resource allocation, risk mitigation, and overall business performance.

2. **Enhanced Risk Management:** A well-implemented GRC framework enables you to identify and manage risks more effectively, reducing the likelihood of security incidents and financial losses. By proactively addressing risks, you can safeguard your organisation's assets and ensure business continuity.
3. **Regulatory Compliance:** Ensuring compliance with regulations protects your organisation from legal penalties and builds trust with customers, partners, and stakeholders. A comprehensive GRC programme helps you stay ahead of regulatory changes and ensures that your organisation operates within the bounds of the law.
4. **Increased Efficiency:** By streamlining processes and reducing redundancies, a coordinated GRC approach can significantly increase operational efficiency. This allows your organisation to focus on its core activities while maintaining a strong security posture.
5. **Stronger Organisational Culture:** Embedding GRC principles into your organisational culture creates an environment where security and compliance are valued by all employees. This leads to greater accountability, better adherence to policies, and a more resilient organisation.

Conclusion

Governance, Risk, and Compliance are critical components of a secure and resilient organisation. By establishing a robust GRC framework, you can ensure that your security efforts are aligned with your business objectives, risks are managed proactively, and compliance with regulations is maintained. As the regulatory environment becomes more complex and cyber threats continue to evolve, a strong GRC programme is essential for protecting your organisation and ensuring its long-term success.

In the next chapter, we'll explore the role of the Security Operations Centre (SOC) in monitoring and responding to security threats in real time, and discuss how to build and manage an effective SOC to enhance your organisation's security operations

12
Security Operations Centre

Introduction to the Security Operations Centre (SOC)

No matter where you look in the global digital landscape, cyber threats are not only pervasive but also increasingly sophisticated, the Security Operations Centre (SOC) is an indispensable component of an organisation's cybersecurity strategy. The SOC acts as the central hub for monitoring, detecting, and responding to security incidents in real time, serving as the first line of defence against cyber threats.

However, a well-established SOC does much more than react to incidents, it proactively hunts for threats, analyses data for early warning signs, and coordinates responses to minimise damage and facilitate quick recovery. By integrating people, processes, and technology, the SOC ensures that an organisation remains resilient in the face of evolving threats. It's where all aspects of security converge, providing a comprehensive and coordinated approach to protecting your organisation's assets, data, and reputation.

In this chapter, we'll delve into the critical functions of a SOC, explore the detailed team structure, discuss the essential technologies that underpin its success, and examine the challenges faced by SOCs along with strategies to overcome them. We'll also cover how to continuously improve and optimise your SOC to keep pace with the ever-changing threat landscape.

Understanding the Role of the SOC

The SOC is the nerve centre of an organisation's cybersecurity efforts, providing continuous surveillance and rapid response to security incidents. But beyond reacting to threats, a mature SOC plays a

DOI: 10.1201/9781003585923-12

proactive role in threat hunting, forensic analysis, and strategic security planning.

Key Functions of the SOC

1. **Continuous Monitoring:** The SOC operates 24/7, constantly scanning the organisation's networks, systems, and applications for signs of malicious activity. This includes collecting and analysing logs, network traffic, and system alerts from across the IT infrastructure.
2. **Threat Detection and Analysis:** SOC analysts identify and understand security threats, determining the nature, scope, and potential impact of an attack. This involves correlating data, leveraging threat intelligence, and using advanced analytics to detect suspicious behaviour.
3. **Incident Response and Management:** When a security incident occurs, the SOC takes immediate action to mitigate its effects. This includes containing the threat, eradicating malicious elements, and initiating recovery procedures to restore normal operations while minimising business disruption.
4. **Proactive Threat Hunting:** A proactive SOC actively searches for threats that may have bypassed traditional security measures. This involves using advanced analytics, behavioural analysis, and threat intelligence to identify and neutralise threats before they can cause harm.
5. **Forensic Investigation and Root Cause Analysis:** After an incident is contained, the SOC conducts forensic investigations to understand how the breach occurred, what systems were affected, and what data may have been compromised. This analysis is crucial for improving defences and preventing future incidents.
6. **Reporting and Continuous Improvement:** The SOC plays a vital role in communicating security status to stakeholders through detailed reports and dashboards. These reports provide insights into the current threat landscape, the effectiveness of security controls, and areas needing improvement. Regular reviews and updates ensure that the SOC evolves alongside emerging threats.

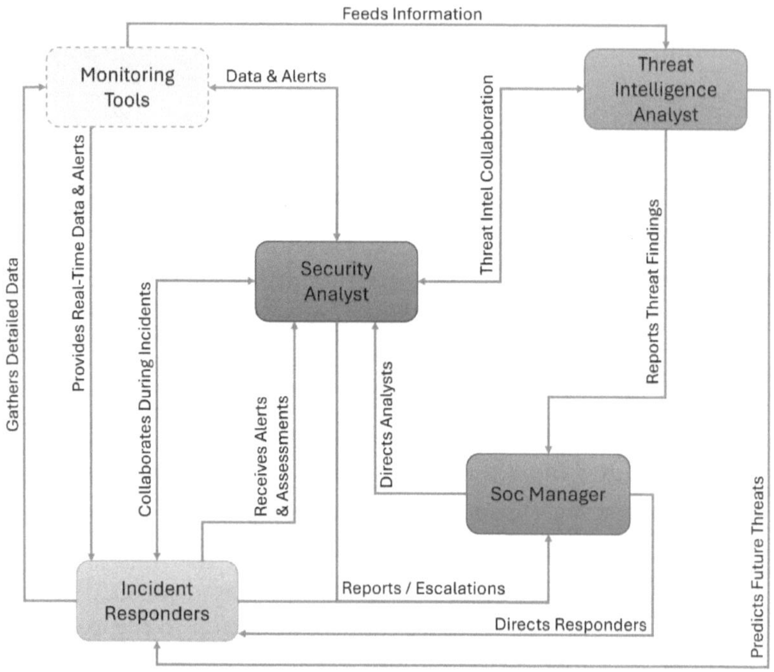

Figure 12.1 Simplified diagram of the security operations centre (SOC) structure, illustrating roles, tools, and the flow of information within the SOC.

Detailed SOC Team Structure

The effectiveness of a SOC heavily relies on its team structure, which typically includes a mix of different roles, each with specific responsibilities (Figure 12.1). A well-defined hierarchy and clear communication flow are essential for the SOC to function efficiently.

Key Roles in a SOC

1. SOC Manager
   - **Responsibilities:** The SOC manager oversees the entire SOC operation, ensuring that all processes run smoothly. They are responsible for strategic planning, managing resources, and ensuring that the SOC meets its objectives.
   - **Interaction:** The SOC manager coordinates with executive leadership, IT, and other departments to align the SOC's activities with the organisation's overall security strategy.

2. Tier 1 Analysts (Alert Analysts)
   - **Responsibilities:** Tier 1 analysts are the first responders who monitor alerts generated by security tools. They perform initial triage, determine whether an alert represents a real threat, and escalate incidents as necessary.
   - **Interaction:** Tier 1 analysts work closely with Tier 2 analysts, escalating potential incidents for further investigation.
3. Tier 2 Analysts (Incident Responders)
   - **Responsibilities:** Tier 2 analysts take over incidents escalated by Tier 1 analysts. They conduct a deeper analysis, determine the scope and impact of the incident, and initiate containment and remediation efforts.
   - **Interaction:** They collaborate with Tier 1 analysts for context and Tier 3 analysts for complex or high-impact incidents.
4. Tier 3 Analysts (Threat Hunters/Advanced Incident Responders)
   - **Responsibilities:** Tier 3 analysts are the most experienced and handle the most complex threats. They engage in threat hunting, conduct forensic investigations, and deal with persistent or sophisticated threats.
   - **Interaction:** They work closely with threat intelligence teams and are often involved in strategic planning and improving detection capabilities.
5. Threat Hunters
   - **Responsibilities:** Threat hunters proactively search for hidden threats within the network, focusing on uncovering advanced persistent threats (APTs) and other sophisticated attacks that evade standard detection methods.
   - **Interaction:** They collaborate with Tier 3 analysts and threat intelligence teams to refine hunting techniques and tools.
6. Forensic Experts
   - **Responsibilities:** Forensic experts analyse compromised systems to understand the full scope of an attack, including identifying the methods used by attackers and the data accessed or stolen.

- **Interaction:** They work with Tier 3 analysts to provide detailed forensic reports that inform incident response and future prevention strategies.

7. SOC Engineers/Tool Administrators
    - **Responsibilities:** SOC engineers manage and maintain the technology stack used by the SOC, ensuring that all tools are operational and integrated effectively.
    - **Interaction:** They support all analyst tiers by maintaining the tools that analysts rely on for threat detection and incident response.

Steps to Build an Effective SOC

1. **Define the SOC's Mission and Objectives:** The first step in building a SOC is to clearly define its mission and objectives. This includes determining the specific threats the SOC will address, the assets it will protect, and the level of service it will provide (e.g., 24/7 coverage vs. business hours only).
2. **Assemble a Skilled SOC Team:** A SOC is only as strong as the team that operates it. Assembling a team of skilled professionals, including security analysts, incident responders, and threat hunters, is crucial. Each team member should have clearly defined roles and responsibilities, with ongoing training to keep their skills sharp.
3. **Deploy the Right Technologies:** The effectiveness of a SOC relies heavily on the technologies it uses. Key technologies include SIEM systems, Intrusion Detection and Prevention Systems (IDS/IPS), Endpoint Detection and Response (EDR) tools, and threat intelligence platforms. These technologies provide the data, context, and automation needed for effective threat detection and response.
4. **Develop and Document Standard Operating Procedures (SOPs):** To ensure consistent and effective operations, it's critical to develop and document Standard Operating Procedures (SOPs) for all SOC activities. SOPs should cover everything from initial threat detection to full-scale incident response and post-incident analysis.

5. **Implement Threat Intelligence and Analysis:** Integrating threat intelligence into SOC operations enables the team to stay ahead of emerging threats. This involves subscribing to threat intelligence feeds, analysing global threat data, and using this information to fine-tune detection and response efforts.
6. **Establish Strong Communication and Collaboration Channels:** The SOC must maintain strong communication and collaboration channels with other departments, including IT, legal, compliance, and executive management. This ensures that security efforts are coordinated across the organisation and that the SOC has the support it needs to respond effectively to incidents.
7. **Focus on Continuous Training and Skill Development:** The threat landscape is constantly evolving, making continuous training and skill development essential for SOC staff. This includes not only technical training but also simulations and exercises to improve the team's readiness to handle real-world incidents.

Essential SOC Technologies

The SOC relies on a robust technology stack to detect, analyse, and respond to threats effectively. These technologies must be integrated to provide a comprehensive view of the organisation's security posture and enable efficient operations.

Key Technologies in a SOC

1. Security Information and Event Management (SIEM)
   - **Functionality:** SIEM systems are the backbone of SOC operations, aggregating and analysing data from across the IT environment. They correlate logs and events from multiple sources to detect anomalies and generate alerts for further investigation.
2. Extended Detection and Response (XDR)
   - **Functionality:** XDR extends the capabilities of traditional detection tools by integrating and correlating data across multiple security layers, including endpoints, networks,

servers, and email systems. XDR provides a unified view of the threat landscape, enhancing the SOC's ability to detect, investigate, and respond to sophisticated attacks.

3. Security Orchestration, Automation, and Response (SOAR)
   - **Functionality:** SOAR platforms automate routine tasks like alert triage and incident response, reducing the time needed to respond to incidents. SOAR also ensures that responses are consistent and aligned with predefined playbooks, enhancing operational efficiency.
4. Intrusion Detection and Prevention Systems (IDS/IPS)
   - **Functionality:** IDS/IPS tools monitor network traffic for signs of malicious activity. IDS systems alert the SOC to potential threats, while IPS systems can take automated actions to block or mitigate these threats.
5. Endpoint Detection and Response (EDR)
   - **Functionality:** EDR solutions provide visibility into endpoint activities, helping the SOC detect and respond to threats that bypass network defences. EDR tools allow for the isolation of compromised devices and detailed analysis of endpoint-level incidents.
6. Threat Intelligence Platforms:
   - **Functionality:** These platforms provide the SOC with up-to-date information on global threats, enabling more informed decision-making. By integrating threat intelligence into SIEM, XDR, and SOAR systems, SOCs can enhance their ability to detect emerging threats.
7. Log Management Systems
   - **Functionality:** Log management is critical for SOC operations, providing a historical record of all system activities. Logs are essential for forensic investigations and compliance reporting and are often integrated with SIEM systems for real-time analysis.

The Role of Automation and AI in SOC Operations

Automation and artificial intelligence (AI) have become increasingly important in modern SOCs, helping to manage the vast amounts of data generated by security tools and enhancing the speed and accuracy of threat detection and response.

Benefits of Automation and AI

1. Enhanced Threat Detection
    - AI-driven analytics can process and analyse data far faster than humans, identifying patterns and anomalies that might indicate a threat. Machine learning models can be trained to recognise both known and emerging threats, improving the SOC's detection capabilities.
2. Automated Incident Response
    - Automation tools, such as SOAR platforms, can automatically execute predefined response actions when certain conditions are met, such as isolating infected systems or blocking malicious IP addresses. This reduces response times and ensures consistency in how incidents are handled.
3. Reduction of False Positives
    - AI can help reduce the number of false positives by filtering out benign activities that might otherwise trigger alerts. Machine learning models refine their accuracy over time, ensuring that analysts are only alerted to genuine threats.

Challenges and Pitfalls

1. Over-reliance on Automation
    - While automation can significantly enhance efficiency, there's a risk of becoming overly reliant on it. Some threats, especially those that are subtle or novel, may require human intuition and expertise to identify and analyse.
2. AI Bias and Errors
    - AI systems are only as good as the data they are trained on. If the training data is incomplete or biased, the AI may make incorrect assumptions, leading to missed threats or unnecessary alerts.

Challenges in SOC Operations

Operating a SOC comes with its own set of challenges. Understanding these challenges is key to overcoming them and ensuring that the SOC remains effective.

Common Challenges

1. Alert Fatigue
    - SOC analysts can become overwhelmed by the sheer volume of alerts generated by security tools, leading to fatigue and potentially missing critical incidents.
2. False Positives
    - A significant portion of alerts can turn out to be false positives, consuming valuable time and resources that could be better spent on genuine threats.
3. Data Overload
    - The SOC must process massive amounts of data from across the organisation's IT environment. Managing and analysing this data effectively is a major challenge.
4. Sophisticated Threats
    - Advanced Persistent Threats (APTs) and other sophisticated attacks can be difficult to detect and respond to, especially if they are designed to evade traditional security measures.

Strategies to Overcome SOC Challenges

1. Managing Alert Fatigue
    - Implement machine learning models to prioritise alerts based on risk, allowing analysts to focus on the most critical threats.
    - Regularly refine detection rules to reduce unnecessary alerts.
2. Reducing False Positives
    - Use advanced analytics and threat intelligence to filter out benign activities and improve the accuracy of threat detection.

- Continuously train machine learning models with updated data to enhance their accuracy.

3. Handling Data Overload
   - Implement log management systems and SIEM tools that can efficiently process and correlate large volumes of data.
   - Prioritise data sources that provide the most valuable insights, such as endpoints and network traffic, and focus on integrating them into your SIEM and XDR platforms.
4. Detecting and Responding to Sophisticated Threats
   - Invest in advanced technologies like XDR and behavioural analytics to detect sophisticated threats.
   - Engage in proactive threat hunting to identify and neutralise threats before they can cause harm.

Measuring SOC Effectiveness

To ensure that the SOC remains effective, it's important to measure its performance using key metrics and KPIs.

Key Performance Indicators (KPIs) and Metrics

1. Mean Time to Detect (MTTD)
   - The average time it takes for the SOC to detect a threat after it has occurred. A lower MTTD indicates more efficient threat detection.
2. Mean Time to Respond (MTTR)
   - The average time it takes for the SOC to respond to and mitigate a threat after it has been detected. A lower MTTR indicates a faster and more effective incident response.
3. Incident Closure Rate
   - The percentage of incidents that are fully resolved within a given time frame. A higher closure rate indicates effective incident management.
4. False Positives vs. True Positives
   - The ratio of false positives (alerts that are not genuine threats) to true positives (alerts that represent actual threats). Reducing the number of false positives is crucial for maintaining analyst productivity and focus.

Continuous Improvement through Metrics

Metrics are not just for measuring current performance, they are also tools for driving continuous improvement within the SOC.

Using Metrics for Continuous Improvement

1. Resource Allocation
   - Use MTTD and MTTR metrics to identify areas where additional resources or training might be needed. For example, if MTTR is consistently high, it may indicate a need for more automated response capabilities or additional incident response staff.
2. Technology Investments
   - Analyse the incident closure rate and false positive ratio to determine whether current technologies are effective. If false positives are too high, it may be time to invest in more advanced analytics or machine learning tools.
3. Process Adjustments
   - Regularly review SOPs and adjust them based on performance data. If certain types of incidents consistently take longer to resolve, this might indicate a need to refine or update response procedures.

Conclusion

The Security Operations Centre (SOC) is a critical component of an organisation's cybersecurity strategy, serving as the frontline defence against cyber threats. By providing continuous monitoring, threat detection, and incident response, the SOC ensures that potential threats are identified and addressed before they can cause significant harm.

Building and optimising a SOC requires a strategic approach that combines the right mix of technology, talent, and processes. Once established, a SOC must be continuously refined and improved to keep pace with the evolving threat landscape. By integrating advanced analytics, automation, and threat intelligence, and by fostering collaboration across the organisation, the SOC can remain an effective and essential part of your organisation's security infrastructure.

In the next chapter, we'll explore the critical aspects of Incident Response and Management, delving into the strategies and best practices for effectively managing security incidents and minimising their impact on your organisation.

13
Incident Response and Management

Introduction to Incident Response and Management

Today's cyber threat landscape, where breaches and attacks can occur at any moment, having a robust incident response and management plan is not just a luxury; it's a necessity. The ability to quickly detect, respond to, and recover from security incidents can mean the difference between a minor disruption and a catastrophic breach. Incident Response (IR) is the process of handling security events in a structured and efficient manner, with the goal of minimising damage, preserving evidence, and restoring normal operations as quickly as possible.

Effective incident management is more than just reacting to an incident; it involves a comprehensive approach that includes preparation, detection, analysis, containment, eradication, recovery, and learning. Each of these phases plays a crucial role in ensuring that your organisation can withstand and bounce back from cyberattacks and other security incidents.

In this chapter, we'll explore the essential components of an incident response plan, the phases of incident management, and best practices for building a resilient incident response capability. We'll also delve into the critical role of communication during an incident and how to manage the crisis effectively, ensuring that your organisation's reputation and compliance obligations are maintained.

Understanding the Incident Response Lifecycle

The incident response lifecycle is a structured approach to managing and mitigating security incidents. This lifecycle is typically divided

DOI: 10.1201/9781003585923-13

into six phases: preparation, identification, containment, eradication, recovery, and lessons learned. Each phase is essential to ensuring that incidents are handled efficiently and effectively, minimising the impact on the organisation.

Preparation

Preparation is the foundation of an effective incident response plan. It involves establishing and maintaining the policies, procedures, tools, and resources necessary to respond to incidents swiftly and effectively. The goal is to ensure that your organisation is ready to handle incidents before they occur.

Key Activities in the Preparation Phase

- **Developing an Incident Response Plan (IRP):** The IRP outlines the processes and procedures that will be followed during an incident. This plan should be detailed and cover all aspects of incident management, from detection to recovery.
- **Establishing an Incident Response Team (IRT):** The IRT is a dedicated group of professionals responsible for executing the IRP. This team should include members from various departments, such as IT, legal, communications, and management, to ensure a coordinated response.
- **Training and Awareness:** Regular training ensures that all members of the IRT are familiar with the IRP and their specific roles during an incident. It also helps build a security-aware culture across the organisation.
- **Deploying Incident Detection Tools:** Tools such as SIEM systems, Intrusion Detection Systems (IDS), and Endpoint Detection and Response (EDR) platforms are essential for identifying and alerting the IRT to potential incidents.

Identification

The identification phase involves detecting and recognising potential security incidents. This phase is crucial because the speed and accuracy of identification can significantly impact the effectiveness of the subsequent response.

Key Activities in the Identification Phase

- **Monitoring and Detection:** Continuous monitoring of network traffic, system logs, and user activity is essential for identifying potential incidents. Tools like SIEM systems, IDS/IPS, and EDR platforms play a critical role in this phase.
- **Incident Classification:** Once a potential incident is identified, it must be classified based on its severity, impact, and scope. This classification helps determine the appropriate response.
- **Incident Triage:** Triage involves assessing the incident to determine its nature and scope. This process helps prioritise the response and allocate resources effectively.

Containment

The containment phase focuses on limiting the damage caused by an incident and preventing it from spreading to other parts of the network. Containment strategies can vary depending on the type and severity of the incident.

Key Activities in the Containment Phase

- **Short-Term Containment:** This involves immediate actions to limit the impact of the incident, such as isolating affected systems or blocking malicious IP addresses.
- **Long-Term Containment:** Long-term containment involves implementing temporary fixes to ensure that the incident is fully contained and that business operations can continue while the root cause is being addressed.
- **Communication and Coordination:** During containment, clear communication with all stakeholders is essential. The IRT must coordinate with IT, legal, compliance, and management to ensure that containment efforts are effective and aligned with business priorities.

Eradication

The eradication phase involves removing the root cause of the incident and eliminating any traces of malicious activity from the affected systems. This phase is crucial for ensuring that the threat does not reoccur.

Key Activities in the Eradication Phase

- **Identifying the Root Cause:** To effectively eradicate a threat, the IRT must first identify the root cause of the incident, such as a vulnerability that was exploited or a compromised account.
- **Removing Malicious Components:** All malicious code, files, and processes must be completely removed from the affected systems. This may involve restoring systems from clean backups or using specialised tools to remove malware.
- **Applying Patches and Updates:** Any vulnerabilities that were exploited during the incident must be patched to prevent further exploitation. This may also involve updating security configurations or applying software updates.

Recovery

The recovery phase focuses on restoring normal operations and ensuring that the affected systems are secure and fully functional. This phase includes validating that all systems are clean, applying any necessary security enhancements, and gradually bringing systems back online.

Key Activities in the Recovery Phase

- **System Restoration:** The IRT must ensure that all affected systems are restored to their pre-incident state, using clean backups if necessary. This includes verifying that all malicious components have been removed and that the systems are functioning normally.
- **Validation and Testing:** Before bringing systems back online, the IRT should conduct thorough testing to ensure that the systems are secure and fully operational. This may involve running vulnerability scans, penetration tests, or other assessments.
- **Gradual Reintroduction of Services:** Systems and services should be brought back online in a controlled manner,

prioritising critical systems first. This approach helps ensure that any remaining issues are identified and addressed promptly.

Lessons Learned

The final phase of the incident response lifecycle involves reviewing and analysing the incident to identify lessons learned and improve future response efforts. This phase is critical for continuous improvement and for ensuring that the organisation is better prepared for future incidents.

Key Activities in the Lessons Learned Phase

- **Post-incident Review:** The IRT should conduct a thorough review of the incident, including how it was detected, how the response was managed, and what could have been done better. This review should be documented and shared with relevant stakeholders.
- **Update Incident Response Plan:** Based on the lessons learned, the IRP should be updated to reflect any changes in procedures, technologies, or team responsibilities. This ensures that the plan remains relevant and effective.
- **Training and Awareness:** The lessons learned from the incident should be incorporated into training programmes and awareness campaigns to ensure that all employees are informed and prepared for future incidents.

Communication Protocols during an Incident

Effective communication is one of the most critical elements of incident response. Clear, timely, and accurate communication ensures that everyone involved in the response is informed and aligned, helping to manage the incident more effectively and mitigate its impact.

Internal Communication

- **Incident Briefings:** Regular briefings should be held for the IRT and key stakeholders, including executive management,

IT, legal, and compliance teams. These briefings should provide updates on the status of the incident, the actions being taken, and any new developments.

- **Clear Command Structure:** Establish a clear chain of command for communication. Designate a Single Point Of Contact (SPOC) responsible for coordinating communication within the IRT and with other departments.
- **Documentation and Reporting:** All communications during an incident should be thoroughly documented. This includes decisions made, actions taken, and communications with external parties. This documentation is crucial for post-incident reviews and regulatory reporting.

External Communication

- **Stakeholder Notifications:** Depending on the severity and scope of the incident, it may be necessary to notify customers, partners, vendors, and other stakeholders. Communications should be clear and factual and should convey what actions are being taken to address the incident.
- **Media and Public Relations:** If the incident is significant and could impact the organisation's reputation, a coordinated public relations strategy is essential. This includes preparing press statements, holding media briefings, and managing social media communications.
- **Regulatory Reporting:** Many regulations require organisations to report security incidents to regulatory bodies within a specific timeframe. Ensure that these reports are accurate and that all legal obligations are met.

Maintaining Transparency and Control

- **Transparency:** While it is important to be transparent with stakeholders and the public, it's also crucial to control the narrative. Share necessary information, but avoid disclosing details that could aid attackers or cause undue panic.

- **Consistency:** Ensure that all communications are consistent across all channels. Mixed messages can lead to confusion and damage trust with stakeholders.
- **Preparedness:** Develop pre-approved communication templates and protocols as part of the IRP. This ensures that communication can be swift and consistent during an incident.

Crisis Management

When a security incident escalates into a full-blown crisis, the stakes become even higher. Effective crisis management can prevent a security incident from spiralling into a reputational disaster or a legal nightmare.

Managing Public Relations

- **Crisis Communication Plan:** A crisis communication plan should be an integral part of your overall incident response strategy. This plan should outline how to communicate with the media, stakeholders, and the public during a crisis, including who will speak on behalf of the organisation and what key messages will be conveyed.
- **Media Relations:** In a crisis, the media can be both a challenge and an ally. It's essential to manage media relations proactively, providing timely and accurate information while avoiding speculation or misinformation.
- **Social Media Management:** Social media can amplify a crisis if not managed properly. Monitor social media channels for misinformation or negative sentiment and respond quickly to control the narrative.

Legal Implications

- **Regulatory Compliance:** During a crisis, compliance with regulatory requirements becomes even more critical. This includes timely breach notification, cooperation with investigations, and ensuring that all actions taken are legally defensible.

- **Legal Counsel Involvement:** Involve legal counsel early in the incident response process, especially in the case of potential data breaches or incidents involving sensitive customer information. Legal advisors can provide guidance on compliance, liability, and communications.
- **Documentation for Legal Defence:** Ensure that all actions taken during the incident are well-documented. This documentation may be needed for legal defence, regulatory inquiries, or insurance claims.

Regulatory Reporting

- **Timely Reporting:** Many regulations have strict timelines for reporting security incidents. Ensure that your IRP includes protocols for identifying incidents that require regulatory reporting and for meeting those deadlines.
- **Accurate Reporting:** Reports to regulators should be accurate and complete. Inaccurate or incomplete reporting can lead to penalties, fines, or further investigations.
- **Cooperation with Regulators:** Be prepared to cooperate fully with regulators during and after a crisis. This may include providing additional information, participating in audits, or implementing corrective actions.

Building a Resilient Incident Response Capability

Building a resilient incident response capability requires more than just a documented plan. It involves creating a culture of preparedness, investing in the right tools and technologies, and ensuring that the entire organisation is aligned and ready to respond to incidents.

Key Components of a Resilient Incident Response Capability

1. **Strong Leadership and Governance:** Effective incident response requires strong leadership and governance. Senior management must be committed to supporting the incident response function, providing the necessary resources, and

ensuring that the IRP is aligned with the organisation's strategic objectives.

2. **Skilled and Experienced Incident Response Team:** The effectiveness of the incident response function depends on the skills and experience of the IRT. The team should be composed of individuals with expertise in various areas, including network security, digital forensics, malware analysis, and legal compliance.
3. **Advanced Detection and Response Tools:** The tools and technologies used by the IRT are critical to the success of the incident response function. These tools should provide real-time visibility into the organisation's IT environment, enabling the team to detect and respond to incidents quickly and effectively.
4. **Regular Testing and Drills:** Incident response plans should be regularly tested through tabletop exercises, simulations, and live drills. These tests help ensure that the IRT is prepared to handle real-world incidents and that the IRP is effective.
5. **Continuous Improvement and Adaptation:** The threat landscape is constantly evolving, and the incident response function must adapt to keep pace. Continuous improvement involves regularly reviewing and updating the IRP, incorporating lessons learned from past incidents, and staying informed about emerging threats and best practices.

Conclusion

Incident response and management are critical components of any organisation's cybersecurity strategy. By preparing for incidents, responding swiftly and effectively, and continuously improving your incident response capabilities, you can minimise the impact of security incidents and protect your organisation from the growing threat of cyberattacks.

Building a resilient incident response function requires strong leadership, skilled personnel, advanced tools, and a commitment to continuous improvement. By following the best practices outlined in this chapter and integrating incident response into your overall security strategy, you can ensure that your organisation is prepared to handle any security challenge that comes its way.

In the next chapter, we'll explore Security Automation and Orchestration, examining how automation can streamline and enhance your security operations, enabling faster and more effective responses to threats.

14
Security Automation and Orchestration

Introduction to Security Automation and Orchestration

As cyber threats grow in complexity and volume, traditional security operations increasingly struggle to keep pace. Manual processes, while effective in specific scenarios, can be slow, prone to errors, and resource-intensive. Security Automation and Orchestration (SA&O) have emerged as critical tools to enhance the efficiency, speed, and consistency of security operations, enabling organisations to respond to threats more effectively.

Security Automation refers to the use of technology to perform tasks without human intervention, speeding up processes and reducing the burden on security teams. Orchestration involves integrating and coordinating multiple security tools and processes to work together seamlessly. Together, these technologies empower organisations to detect and respond to threats swiftly, while allowing human resources to focus on more strategic and complex tasks.

Yet, SA&O's impact extends beyond the Security Operations Centre (SOC). When implemented thoughtfully, automation and orchestration can transform various facets of IT operations and business processes, enhancing an organisation's overall security posture and operational resilience.

The Expanding Role of Security Automation and Orchestration

Security Automation and Orchestration address several critical challenges that modern organisations encounter, particularly as the complexity and volume of cyber threats continue to grow. One of the biggest issues faced today is the overwhelming number of security

DOI: 10.1201/9781003585923-14

alerts that teams must manage on a daily basis. With so many potential threats to track, it's easy for genuine risks to be overlooked or for response times to slow down. Automation helps streamline this process by automatically identifying and prioritising threats, reducing the burden on security teams and enabling faster, more efficient responses.

At the same time, regulatory requirements around data protection and cybersecurity have become increasingly stringent. Compliance is no longer optional, and organisations need to ensure that their security operations meet legal and industry standards. Security Orchestration helps coordinate the many tools and systems used across an organisation, ensuring that they work together seamlessly to meet these regulatory requirements. It also standardises processes, ensuring that security protocols are consistently followed, which is essential for passing audits and demonstrating compliance.

As cyber threats continue to evolve in both sophistication and frequency, the need for rapid, well-coordinated responses has never been more important. Automation and orchestration enable organisations to respond in real time, minimising damage and ensuring that security operations can scale effectively alongside the growing threat landscape. These technologies not only enhance operational efficiency but also improve overall resilience, allowing organisations to stay ahead of emerging threats while maintaining compliance and protecting critical assets.

Managing Growing Threats and Data Volumes

The increasing sophistication of cyber threats, combined with the exponential growth of data generated across modern IT environments, has created an urgent need for more efficient, scalable, and responsive security operations. Traditional manual processes are often unable to keep up with this pace, leaving organisations vulnerable to missed threats, prolonged detection times, and delayed responses. The result is greater exposure to risks that can cause significant financial and reputational damage.

This is where automation becomes indispensable. By automating routine security tasks, such as alert triage, log analysis, and even the initial stages of incident response, organisations can drastically reduce the burden on security teams. Automation helps sort through the massive volumes of data that modern systems generate, filtering out low-priority alerts and highlighting the incidents that need immediate attention. This not only improves efficiency but also ensures that critical threats aren't lost in the noise of minor issues or false positives.

Ensuring Consistent and Efficient Responses

One of the major benefits of automation is its ability to ensure consistent and reliable responses to security incidents. In manual processes, responses can vary greatly depending on who is handling the incident, their level of experience, or even the pressure they are under at the time. This variability can lead to inconsistent outcomes, where critical steps might be overlooked, miscommunicated, or delayed, potentially exacerbating the severity of a security breach.

Automation, on the other hand, reduces these human-driven inconsistencies by standardising the process. With automated workflows, predefined protocols and procedures are followed every single time, ensuring that every security incident is managed according to established best practices, regardless of the complexity or time constraints. This approach significantly reduces the risk of human error, ensuring that vital actions, such as quarantining infected systems, notifying relevant stakeholders, or initiating backups, are never missed or delayed.

Scaling Security Operations

For many organisations, especially those operating with limited budgets or small teams, scaling security operations to keep pace with the growing volume and complexity of cyber threats is a daunting challenge. As digital infrastructures expand, so too does the attack surface, leaving organisations increasingly vulnerable to sophisticated and frequent cyberattacks. However, the reality is that scaling security operations through traditional means, such as hiring more staff or manually handling every incident, is often neither feasible nor sustainable. This is particularly true for small to mid-sized organisations, where resources are limited and the cybersecurity skills gap presents an additional obstacle.

This is where automation and orchestration come into play, offering a solution that allows organisations to scale their security operations efficiently and cost-effectively. Automation reduces the need for manual intervention by handling routine, repetitive tasks such as alert triage, log management, and system monitoring. By taking these time-consuming activities off the hands of human analysts, automation frees up valuable resources, enabling teams to focus on higher-priority tasks that require human expertise, such as advanced threat hunting, incident investigation, and strategic decision-making.

Orchestration further enhances this efficiency by integrating and coordinating the various security tools and systems that an organisation uses. It ensures that these tools work together seamlessly, streamlining processes and reducing the potential for gaps in security coverage. By automating workflows and response actions across multiple platforms, orchestration allows security teams to respond to incidents faster and with greater precision, ensuring that even as the organisation grows, its security posture remains robust.

Key Components of Security Automation and Orchestration

Implementing effective SA&O requires a combination of the right technologies, well-defined processes, and seamless integration across the security ecosystem.

Security Orchestration, Automation, and Response (SOAR) Platforms

SOAR platforms are central to any SA&O strategy. They provide a unified interface for managing security incidents, automating responses, and orchestrating actions across multiple security tools. These platforms integrate with a variety of security solutions, such as SIEM, EDR, and threat intelligence platforms, to streamline security operations.

SOAR platforms also enable the automation of incident response playbooks, which define how specific types of incidents should be handled. By automating these workflows, organisations can ensure that incidents are managed efficiently and consistently, reducing the likelihood of errors and improving response times.

Security Information and Event Management (SIEM)

SIEM systems play a crucial role in SA&O by aggregating, correlating, and analysing security data from across an organisation's IT infrastructure. SIEM systems can automatically detect patterns and anomalies in this data, identifying potential security incidents in real time.

When integrated with SOAR platforms, SIEM systems can trigger automated responses to detected threats. This integration allows organisations to respond to incidents more quickly, reducing the potential impact of security breaches.

Extended Detection and Response (XDR)

XDR solutions expand the capabilities of traditional EDR by providing comprehensive visibility across an organisation's entire IT environment, including endpoints, networks, servers, and cloud services. XDR integrates multiple security products into a cohesive system, enhancing threat detection and response capabilities.

By automating the detection and response to threats across different layers of the IT environment, XDR solutions provide a more holistic approach to security, ensuring that no part of the organisation is left vulnerable.

Threat Intelligence Platforms

Threat intelligence platforms enhance the effectiveness of SA&O by providing actionable insights into known threats, vulnerabilities, and attack techniques. Integrating threat intelligence with SOAR, SIEM, and XDR platforms allows organisations to enrich security alerts with contextual information, prioritising responses based on the severity and relevance of the threat.

Threat intelligence also plays a key role in proactive security measures, such as automated threat hunting and continuous updating of security playbooks. By staying informed about the latest threats, organisations can ensure that their automated responses remain effective against evolving attack vectors.

Implementing Security Automation and Orchestration

Successfully implementing SA&O involves careful planning and execution. Organisations must assess their current security operations, define clear objectives, select the right tools, and develop effective automation workflows.

Assessing Current Security Operations

The first step in implementing SA&O is to assess the current state of security operations. This involves identifying bottlenecks, inefficiencies, and areas where manual tasks are causing delays or inconsistencies. By understanding these pain points, organisations can prioritise automation efforts where they will have the most significant impact.

Defining Automation Goals

Clear, measurable goals are essential for guiding the implementation of SA&O. These goals should align with the organisation's overall security strategy and address specific challenges, such as reducing incident response times, improving compliance, or enhancing the scalability of security operations.

Selecting and Integrating Tools

Choosing the right tools is critical for the success of SA&O initiatives. Organisations should select SOAR platforms, SIEM systems, XDR solutions, and threat intelligence platforms that integrate well with their existing security infrastructure. This integration ensures that data flows seamlessly between tools, enabling more effective automation and orchestration.

Developing and Testing Playbooks

Automated playbooks are at the heart of SA&O. These predefined workflows outline the steps to be taken during a security incident, from detection to remediation. Organisations should develop playbooks for common incident types, such as phishing attacks, malware infections, and data breaches, and test them thoroughly to ensure they function as intended.

Continuous Monitoring and Improvement

SA&O is not a set-and-forget solution. Continuous monitoring and improvement are essential to ensure that automated processes remain effective and aligned with the latest threats. Organisations should regularly review the performance of their automation workflows, using metrics such as response times, false positive rates, and incident resolution rates to identify areas for improvement.

Beyond the SOC: Expanding Automation Across IT and Business Processes

While the SOC is a natural starting point for automation, the benefits of SA&O extend to other areas of IT and business operations.

Patch Management

Automation can streamline patch management by automatically identifying vulnerable systems, downloading patches, and deploying them across the network. This reduces the window of exposure to known vulnerabilities and ensures compliance with security policies.

Compliance and Audit Reporting

Automation simplifies compliance efforts by automatically collecting and compiling data for regulatory reports. This not only reduces the time and effort required for audits but also ensures accuracy and consistency in reporting.

Identity and Access Management (IAM)

Automation can enhance IAM processes by automatically provisioning and de-provisioning user accounts, enforcing access policies, and monitoring user activities for signs of compromise. This reduces the risk of insider threats and ensures that access controls are consistently applied.

Cloud Security Management

As organisations migrate to the cloud, automation can help manage and secure cloud environments by automatically enforcing security policies, monitoring configurations, and responding to incidents. This ensures that cloud resources are protected without requiring manual oversight.

Addressing Challenges in Security Automation and Orchestration

Implementing SA&O is not without challenges. Organisations must navigate issues such as complexity, integration difficulties, and the risk of over-reliance on automation.

Complexity and Integration

Integrating various security tools into a cohesive automation and orchestration framework can be complex, particularly in large or diverse IT environments. Organisations must ensure that these tools work together seamlessly to avoid creating new vulnerabilities or inefficiencies.

Balancing Automation and Human Oversight

While automation can greatly enhance efficiency, over-reliance on it can lead to complacency. Not all threats can be effectively managed by automation; some require human judgment and intervention. Organisations must strike a balance, using automation to handle routine tasks while ensuring that skilled analysts are available to manage complex or unusual incidents.

Managing Alert Fatigue

Automation can reduce alert fatigue by filtering out false positives, but it must be carefully configured to avoid generating its own set of false alarms. Continuous refinement of automation rules and playbooks, informed by real-world data and feedback, is essential to maintain the effectiveness of SA&O.

Conclusion

Security Automation and Orchestration are powerful tools that can transform the way organisations manage and respond to security incidents. By automating routine tasks, orchestrating workflows, and integrating tools across the security stack, organisations can improve efficiency, reduce response times, and enhance their overall security posture.

However, successful implementation requires careful planning, the right tools, and a commitment to continuous improvement. By understanding the key components, challenges, and broader applications of SA&O, organisations can harness the full potential of these technologies to enhance their security operations and overall business resilience.

In the next chapter, we'll explore how to develop a security-aware culture within your organisation, focusing on strategies for engaging employees, promoting best practices, and ensuring that security is a shared responsibility across all levels.

15
Developing a Security-Aware Culture

Introduction to Security-Aware Culture

With a rapidly evolving cybersecurity landscape, technology alone isn't enough to protect an organisation from threats. The human element often represents the weakest link in the security chain. Even the most advanced systems can be compromised by simple mistakes or a lack of awareness. That's why developing a security-aware culture is critical to the overall success of any security strategy.

A security-aware culture is one where every employee, from top executives to frontline workers, understands the importance of security and their role in maintaining it. It's about embedding security into the fabric of the organisation, ensuring that it's not just the responsibility of the IT department but a shared responsibility across all levels and functions (Figure 15.1). By fostering a security-aware culture, organisations can reduce the risk of breaches, improve compliance, and build a more resilient security posture.

Why a Security-Aware Culture Matters

The importance of a security-aware culture cannot be overstated. With the increasing frequency and sophistication of cyberattacks, organisations must ensure that their employees are equipped to recognise and respond to security threats. A strong security culture helps prevent incidents, supports compliance with regulations, and fosters a proactive approach to security.

DOI: 10.1201/9781003585923-15

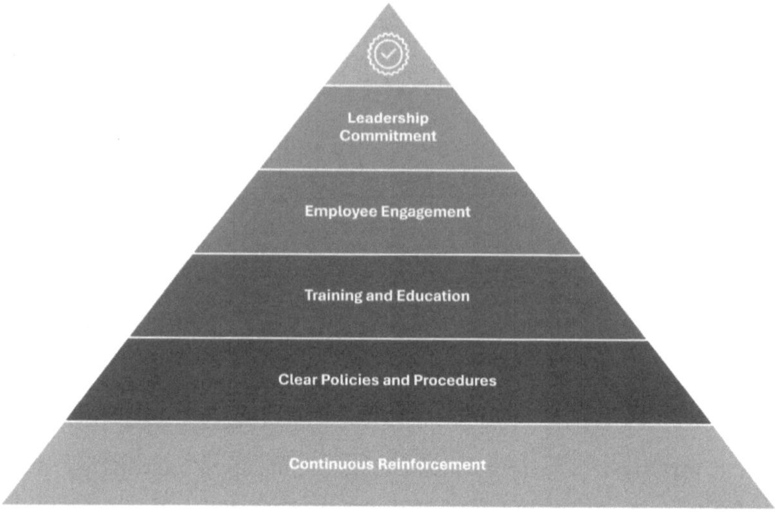

Figure 15.1 A structure pyramid, showing how to build an effective security culture.

Reducing Human Error

Many security incidents result from human errors, such as clicking on phishing links, using weak passwords, or failing to update software. A security-aware culture helps reduce these errors by educating employees about common threats and best practices. By instilling a sense of responsibility and awareness, organisations can significantly lower the chances of these errors leading to serious security breaches.

Supporting Compliance

Regulatory requirements often mandate that organisations implement security awareness training and maintain a culture of security. A security-aware culture helps ensure compliance with laws such as GDPR, HIPAA, and PCI DSS, reducing the risk of fines and legal action. Beyond avoiding penalties, compliance is also about maintaining trust with customers and partners, who expect that their data will be handled with the highest levels of security.

Enhancing Incident Response

When employees are aware of security threats and know how to respond, they can act as the first line of defence, helping to detect and report incidents quickly. This early detection can significantly improve the organisation's ability to contain and mitigate threats. A well-informed workforce is crucial for recognising and responding to potential threats before they escalate into full-blown security incidents.

Building Trust with Customers and Partners

A security-aware culture demonstrates to customers and partners that the organisation takes security seriously. This can enhance trust and improve relationships, leading to stronger business partnerships and customer loyalty. In today's business environment, where data breaches are increasingly common, the assurance that an organisation values and protects its data can be a significant competitive advantage.

Fostering a Proactive Security Posture

A security-aware culture encourages employees to think proactively about security, anticipating potential risks and taking steps to mitigate them. This proactive mindset can lead to better overall security and a more resilient organisation. When employees across all levels are vigilant and proactive about security, it creates an environment where potential risks are identified and addressed before they can cause harm.

Key Components of a Security-Aware Culture

Building a security-aware culture involves several key components: leadership commitment, employee engagement, training and education, clear policies and procedures, continuous reinforcement, and effective communication.

Leadership Commitment

Leadership plays a critical role in establishing and maintaining a security-aware culture. When leaders prioritise security and model good security practices, they set the tone for the entire organisation. Employees look to leadership for cues on what is important, and when security is visibly a priority for leaders, it is more likely to become a priority for the rest of the organisation as well.

Setting the Vision: Leaders should clearly communicate the importance of security and their commitment to fostering a security-aware culture. This vision should be shared with all employees and integrated into the organisation's mission and values. Leadership should articulate how security aligns with the organisation's broader goals and how every employee plays a role in achieving these objectives.

Leading by Example: Leaders should model good security practices in their own behaviour, such as using strong passwords, following secure communication protocols, and participating in security training. This demonstrates that security is important at all levels, not just a concern for the IT department. When executives practice what they preach, it sends a strong message that security is non-negotiable.

Providing Resources: Leadership should ensure that the organisation has the resources necessary to support a security-aware culture, including funding for training programmes, tools for secure communication, and personnel to manage security initiatives. Investing in these resources shows that the organisation is committed to security, and it provides employees with the tools they need to maintain high security standards.

Employee Engagement

Engaging employees in security efforts is essential for building a culture of security. This involves making security relevant to their roles, encouraging active participation, and recognising and rewarding good security behaviour. Engagement goes beyond mandatory training sessions; it's about fostering a genuine interest in security across the organisation.

Making Security Relevant: Tailor security messages and training to the specific roles and responsibilities of employees. This helps them understand how security impacts their daily work and why it's important. For instance, the security concerns of an HR professional will differ from those of a developer or a customer service representative, and training should reflect these differences.

Encouraging Participation: Encourage employees to take an active role in security by reporting suspicious activity, participating in security drills, and suggesting improvements to security processes. This fosters a sense of ownership and responsibility. Employees should feel empowered to contribute to the organisation's security efforts, knowing that their input is valued.

Recognising and Rewarding Good Behaviour: Recognise and reward employees who demonstrate strong security practices or contribute to the organisation's security efforts. This positive reinforcement encourages others to follow suit. Recognition can be formal, such as awards or bonuses, or informal, such as acknowledging efforts in team meetings.

Training and Education

Security awareness training is the cornerstone of a security-aware culture. Effective training programmes provide employees with the knowledge and skills they need to recognise and respond to security threats. Training should not be a one-time event but a continuous process that evolves as new threats emerge.

Regular Training Sessions: Offer regular training sessions to keep employees up to date on the latest security threats, best practices, and policies. Training should be interactive and engaging, using real-world examples and scenarios. This ensures that employees remain vigilant and prepared to handle new challenges.

Role-Specific Training: Provide role-specific training that addresses the unique security risks and responsibilities associated with different positions within the organisation. For example, finance teams might receive training on detecting fraud, while IT staff might focus on preventing data breaches.

Onboarding Training: Integrate security training into the onboarding process for new employees, ensuring that they understand the organisation's security policies and expectations from day one. This sets the tone early and helps new hires recognise that security is a fundamental part of the company culture.

Continuous Learning: Encourage continuous learning by providing access to additional resources, such as online courses, webinars, and industry certifications. This helps employees stay informed and enhances their security expertise. Organisations should create opportunities for employees to deepen their knowledge and stay ahead of emerging threats.

Clear Policies and Procedures

Clear and accessible security policies and procedures are essential for guiding employee behaviour and ensuring that everyone understands their security responsibilities. These policies should be regularly updated to reflect the changing threat landscape and be easily accessible to all employees.

Developing Clear Policies: Create clear, concise, and easily accessible security policies that outline the organisation's expectations for secure behaviour. These policies should cover a wide range of topics, including data protection, access controls, incident reporting, and acceptable use of technology. Policies should be written in plain language to ensure that all employees can understand and follow them.

Communicating Policies: Ensure that security policies are communicated effectively to all employees. This includes regular reminders, updates, and discussions about the importance of following these policies. Communication should be ongoing, not just at the time of policy rollout.

Enforcing Compliance: Enforce compliance with security policies through regular audits, monitoring, and disciplinary actions if necessary. Consistent enforcement reinforces the importance of security and ensures that policies are followed. Employees should be aware that violations of security policies will be taken seriously and could have consequences.

Continuous Reinforcement

Building a security-aware culture is not a one-time effort, it requires ongoing reinforcement to ensure that security remains top of mind for all employees. Continuous reinforcement is key to maintaining the effectiveness of security awareness over time.

Regular Communication: Keep security front and centre through regular communication, such as newsletters, email reminders, and posters. These communications should reinforce key security messages and provide updates on the latest threats and best practices. Regular communication helps ensure that security remains a daily consideration for all employees.

Security Drills and Simulations: Conduct regular security drills and simulations to reinforce training and ensure that employees are prepared to respond to real-world incidents. These exercises help build muscle memory and improve overall readiness. For example, phishing simulations can help employees practice identifying and reporting suspicious emails.

Feedback and Improvement: Encourage feedback from employees on the organisation's security practices and use this feedback to continuously improve the security programme. This creates a sense of ownership and ensures that the programme remains relevant and effective. Employees should feel that their input is valued and that they have a role in shaping the organisation's security culture.

Communication: The Backbone of a Security-Aware Culture

Effective communication is essential for maintaining a security-aware culture. Internally, communication should focus on keeping employees informed about the latest security threats, best practices, and policy updates. Externally, communication is crucial during and after a security incident to manage public relations, legal implications, and regulatory reporting.

Internal Communication: Internal communication is the foundation of a security-aware culture. Regular updates, reminders, and educational materials help keep security top of mind for employees. This can be achieved through various channels, such as newsletters, intranet posts, and team meetings. The goal is to make security a regular topic of discussion, not just something that's addressed during annual training.

External Communication: In the event of a security incident, clear and timely communication with external stakeholders is critical. This includes customers, partners, regulatory bodies, and the media. Organisations must balance the need for transparency with the need to control the narrative and protect their reputation. A well-prepared communication plan can help manage the fallout from an incident, ensuring that stakeholders are informed and reassured.

Sustaining a Security-Aware Culture

Sustaining a security-aware culture over time requires ongoing effort and a commitment to continuous improvement. As the organisation evolves, so too must its security culture, ensuring that security remains a priority even as new challenges and opportunities arise.

Adapting to Change

As the organisation grows and changes, its security needs will evolve. Regularly review and update security policies, training programmes, and communication strategies to ensure they remain relevant and effective. The security landscape is dynamic, and a static security program will quickly become outdated.

Flexibility: Organisations must remain flexible and willing to adapt their security programs as new threats emerge and as their business environment changes. This might involve adopting new technologies, updating policies, or refining training programmes.

Regular Reviews: Conduct regular reviews of the security program to identify areas for improvement. This could involve surveys, audits, or feedback sessions with employees. Regular reviews help ensure that the security program remains effective and relevant.

Maintaining Leadership Commitment: Ensure that leadership continues to prioritise security and model good security practices. This ongoing commitment from the top helps reinforce the importance of security and ensures that it remains a key focus across the organisation.

Continuous Involvement: Leadership should remain actively involved in the organisation's security efforts, attending training sessions, participating in security drills, and staying informed about the latest threats and trends. Their involvement signals to the rest of the organisation that security is a top priority.

Budget and Resources: Leaders should ensure that sufficient budget and resources are allocated to the organisation's security efforts. This includes funding for training programmes, security tools, and personnel. Investing in security sends a clear message that it is a top priority.

Encouraging Innovation: Encourage employees to think creatively about security and to develop innovative solutions to emerging threats. This proactive approach helps keep the organisation ahead of the curve and fosters a culture of continuous improvement.

Innovation Challenges: Organisations can hold innovation challenges or hackathons focused on security, encouraging employees to come up with new ideas for improving the organisation's security posture. This not only generates fresh ideas but also engages employees in the security process.

Employee-Led Initiatives: Encourage employees to take ownership of security initiatives, such as creating new training materials, developing security tools, or leading awareness campaigns. Employee-led initiatives can help drive innovation and create a sense of ownership.

Measuring Success: Regularly measure the success of your security-aware culture by tracking key metrics, such as the number of security incidents, employee participation in training, and compliance with security policies. Use this data to identify areas for improvement and to celebrate successes.

Key Metrics: Metrics can include the number of reported phishing attempts, completion rates for security training, compliance audit results, and the number of security incidents. These metrics provide valuable insights into the effectiveness of the security program.

Continuous Improvement: Use the data collected to continuously refine and improve the security program. This could involve updating training materials, revising policies, or implementing new security measures. Continuous improvement is key to maintaining an effective security program.

Celebrating Success: Recognise and celebrate successes in the security program. This could involve acknowledging departments or individuals who have demonstrated strong security practices or who have contributed to improving the organisation's security posture.

Conclusion

Developing a security-aware culture is essential for protecting your organisation from cyber threats. By engaging employees, providing tailored training, and continuously reinforcing security messages, you can create a culture where security is everyone's responsibility. A security-aware culture not only reduces the risk of incidents but also enhances compliance, builds trust with customers and partners, and fosters a proactive approach to security.

Sustaining this culture requires ongoing effort, leadership commitment, and a willingness to adapt to changing circumstances. By following the best practices outlined in this chapter and making security a core value of your organisation, you can build a more resilient and secure future.

16

Preparing for Cybersecurity Careers

Introduction to Cybersecurity Careers

As the global digital landscape continues to evolve at an unprecedented pace, the demand for skilled cybersecurity professionals has reached new heights. Cybersecurity has emerged as one of the most critical fields in the modern world, with organisations across all industries seeking experts who can safeguard their digital assets, data, and infrastructure from an ever-growing array of threats. Whether you're at the beginning of your career, transitioning from another field, or seeking to deepen your expertise, understanding the skills, certifications, and career paths available in cybersecurity is essential to thriving in this dynamic environment.

The cybersecurity profession is vast, encompassing a wide range of roles from highly technical positions like security analysts and penetration testers to strategic leadership roles such as Chief Information Security Officers (CISOs). Each role demands a unique set of skills and knowledge, and the career path you choose will depend on your interests, strengths, and long-term goals.

In this chapter, we'll delve deeply into the skills necessary for a successful cybersecurity career, explore the certifications that can validate your expertise, and examine the various career paths available in the field. Additionally, we'll discuss strategies for breaking into cybersecurity and advancing your career, ensuring that you are well-prepared to meet the challenges and seize the opportunities that lie ahead.

DOI: 10.1201/9781003585923-16

The Expanding Cybersecurity Landscape

The cybersecurity landscape is continuously expanding and becoming more complex. As digital transformation accelerates across industries, the attack surface for potential cyber threats also grows. This has led to a diversification of roles within cybersecurity, each focusing on specific aspects of protecting an organisation's digital ecosystem. Understanding these roles and how they interconnect is crucial for anyone looking to build a career in cybersecurity.

Core Areas of Cybersecurity

1. **Security Operations:** Security operations are at the heart of an organisation's cybersecurity efforts, responsible for the real-time monitoring, detection, and response to security incidents. Professionals working in Security Operations Centres (SOCs) are tasked with maintaining the security posture of an organisation's IT environment, often working around the clock to protect against threats.
   - **Key Focus:** Continuous monitoring, incident response, threat detection, and maintaining operational security.
   - **Career Progression:** SOC Analyst → Senior Security Analyst → SOC Manager → Director of Security Operations.
2. **Penetration Testing and Ethical Hacking:** Penetration testing, also known as ethical hacking, involves simulating cyberattacks to identify and exploit vulnerabilities in systems, networks, and applications. Ethical hackers play a critical role in helping organisations understand their weaknesses before malicious attackers can exploit them.
   - **Key Focus:** Vulnerability assessment, exploitation techniques, and security testing.
   - **Career Progression:** Junior Penetration Tester → Senior Penetration Tester → Lead Ethical Hacker → Red Team Lead.
3. **Governance, Risk, and Compliance (GRC):** GRC professionals ensure that an organisation's cybersecurity practices are aligned with regulatory requirements, industry standards,

and business objectives. They develop policies, conduct risk assessments, and manage compliance initiatives to ensure that the organisation meets its legal and ethical obligations.

- **Key Focus:** Policy development, risk management, regulatory compliance, and auditing.
- **Career Progression:** GRC Analyst → Senior GRC Analyst → Risk Manager → Director of GRC.

4. **Cybersecurity Engineering:** Cybersecurity engineers design, implement, and manage security solutions that protect an organisation's infrastructure. This includes deploying technologies such as firewalls, Intrusion Detection Systems (IDS), and encryption protocols to safeguard data and prevent unauthorised access.
   - **Key Focus:** Network security, system hardening, encryption, and security infrastructure design.
   - **Career Progression:** Security Engineer → Senior Security Engineer → Security Architect → Chief Security Engineer.
5. **Incident Response and Forensics:** Incident response professionals are the first responders to security breaches. They manage the containment and mitigation of security incidents and conduct forensic investigations to determine the root cause. Their work is critical in preventing future incidents and improving an organisation's overall security posture.
   - **Key Focus:** Incident management, digital forensics, malware analysis, and post-incident review.
   - **Career Progression:** Incident Responder → Senior Incident Responder → Incident Response Team Lead → Director of Incident Response.
6. **Cybersecurity Architecture:** Cybersecurity architects are responsible for designing and overseeing the implementation of an organisation's comprehensive security strategy. They ensure that security measures are integrated into the overall IT infrastructure and aligned with business objectives, often working closely with senior management.
   - **Key Focus:** Security architecture design, strategic planning, and aligning security with business goals.

- **Career Progression:** Security Architect → Enterprise Security Architect → Chief Security Architect → CISO.

7. **Leadership and Management:** Leadership roles in cybersecurity involve setting the security strategy, managing teams, and ensuring that security initiatives align with the organisation's overall business objectives. These roles require a mix of technical knowledge, business acumen, and leadership skills.
   - **Key Focus:** Strategic planning, team leadership, policy development, and communication with stakeholders.
   - **Career Progression:** Security Manager → Director of Cybersecurity → Vice President of Security → CISO.

The Evolution of Cybersecurity Skills

As the cybersecurity landscape evolves, so too do the skills required to succeed in the field. While the foundational technical skills remain crucial, there is an increasing emphasis on a broader set of competencies, including soft skills and strategic thinking. Here, we explore the critical skills needed for a cybersecurity career, both technical and non-technical, and how these skills apply across different roles.

Technical Skills

- **Networking Fundamentals:** Understanding the intricacies of networking is a foundational skill in cybersecurity. This includes knowledge of protocols such as TCP/IP, DNS, and routing, which are essential for securing and managing network traffic.
- **Operating Systems:** Proficiency in managing and securing various operating systems, particularly Windows, Linux, and macOS, is crucial. Cybersecurity professionals must be adept at configuring, troubleshooting, and securing these systems to protect against threats.
- **Scripting and Programming:** Scripting and programming skills are increasingly important in cybersecurity. Proficiency in languages like Python, PowerShell, and Bash allows

professionals to automate tasks, analyse malware, and develop security tools.

- **Threat Intelligence and Analysis:** The ability to analyse threat intelligence is essential for staying ahead of cyber threats. This involves understanding the Tactics, Techniques, and Procedures (TTPs) used by attackers and applying this knowledge to protect the organisation.
- **Risk Management:** Effective risk management involves identifying potential threats, assessing their impact, and implementing controls to mitigate risks. This skill is critical for protecting an organisation's assets and ensuring business continuity.
- **Security Frameworks and Standards:** Familiarity with security frameworks such as NIST, ISO 27001, and CIS Controls is important for aligning an organisation's security practices with industry standards and regulatory requirements.

Soft Skills

- **Problem-Solving:** Cybersecurity professionals must be able to think critically and creatively to solve complex security challenges. This includes developing strategies to protect against and respond to cyber threats in a constantly changing environment.
- **Communication:** Clear and effective communication is essential for explaining technical concepts to non-technical stakeholders, writing reports, and collaborating across teams. Cybersecurity professionals often need to convey risks and solutions to a diverse audience.
- **Attention to Detail:** A high level of attention to detail is required in cybersecurity, as even minor oversights can lead to significant vulnerabilities. This skill is critical in tasks such as code review, log analysis, and policy development.
- **Adaptability:** The cybersecurity landscape is dynamic, with new threats and technologies emerging regularly. Professionals must be adaptable and continuously update their skills to stay ahead of the curve.

- **Ethical Judgment:** Cybersecurity professionals are entrusted with protecting sensitive data and systems. High ethical standards and sound judgment are essential, especially when conducting activities like penetration testing or handling incident response.

The Importance of Certifications in Cybersecurity

Certifications are a key component of career development in cybersecurity. They serve as a formal recognition of your expertise and can significantly enhance your career prospects. Certifications demonstrate your commitment to the field and validate your skills to employers, making them an important factor in hiring and career advancement.

Valuable Cybersecurity Certifications

1. **Certified Information Systems Security Professional (CISSP):** Recognised globally, CISSP is one of the most respected certifications in the industry. It covers a broad range of cybersecurity topics, making it suitable for those aspiring to leadership roles in security management.
2. **Certified Ethical Hacker (CEH):** CEH is focused on ethical hacking and penetration testing. It is designed for professionals who want to develop skills in identifying and exploiting vulnerabilities in systems, networks, and applications.
3. **CompTIA Security+:** As an entry-level certification, Security+ provides a solid foundation in cybersecurity concepts, tools, and best practices. It is ideal for those new to the field, offering a broad overview of essential security topics.
4. **Certified Information Security Manager (CISM):** CISM is aimed at professionals in management roles who are responsible for overseeing an organisation's information security program. It covers risk management, governance, and incident response.
5. **Certified Information Systems Auditor (CISA):** CISA focuses on auditing, control, and assurance of information systems. It is ideal for professionals who specialise in IT auditing, control, and security assessment.

6. **GIAC Security Essentials Certification (GSEC):** GSEC is designed for professionals who want to validate their practical skills and knowledge of information security. It goes beyond basic concepts, requiring a deep understanding of real-world security scenarios.
7. **Certified Cloud Security Professional (CCSP):** CCSP is focused on cloud security, covering topics such as cloud architecture, data security, and compliance. It is ideal for professionals responsible for securing cloud environments and services.

Mapping Out Cybersecurity Career Paths

The diversity of roles within cybersecurity means that professionals can choose from a variety of career paths, each offering unique opportunities and challenges. Whether you're drawn to hands-on technical work, policy and compliance, or leadership and strategy, there's a path that can align with your career aspirations.

Career Pathways

1. **Security Analyst:** Security Analysts monitor and protect an organisation's IT environment, focusing on threat detection and incident response. This role often serves as an entry point into the cybersecurity field, with opportunities to advance to senior analyst positions or management roles.
2. **Penetration Tester:** Penetration Testers simulate cyberattacks to identify vulnerabilities in systems and networks. This role requires strong technical skills and offers a clear pathway to more advanced positions in ethical hacking or security consulting.
3. **Security Engineer:** Security Engineers design and implement security solutions to protect an organisation's infrastructure. This role is highly technical and can lead to advanced positions in security architecture or engineering leadership.
4. **GRC Analyst:** GRC Analysts focus on governance, risk, and compliance, ensuring that an organisation's security practices align with regulatory requirements and business goals. This

role offers opportunities to advance into risk management or compliance leadership positions.

5. **Incident Responder:** Incident Responders manage and mitigate security incidents, playing a critical role in protecting an organisation from cyber threats. With experience, they can move into leadership roles within incident response teams or broader security operations.
6. **Security Architect:** Security Architects design and oversee the implementation of an organisation's security strategy. This role requires a combination of technical expertise and strategic thinking, with opportunities to advance to enterprise architecture or CISO roles.
7. **Chief Information Security Officer (CISO):** The CISO is responsible for the overall security strategy of an organisation. This executive role involves managing teams, budgets, and aligning security initiatives with business objectives. It represents the pinnacle of a cybersecurity career.

Strategies for Breaking into Cybersecurity

Breaking into cybersecurity can be challenging, especially for those transitioning from other fields. However, with the right strategies and mindset, you can build the skills and experience needed to start a successful career in this dynamic field.

Getting Started

- **Build a Strong Foundation:** Start with the basics by gaining a solid understanding of IT fundamentals, including networking, operating systems, and basic security concepts. This foundation is essential for more advanced cybersecurity topics.
- **Pursue Certifications:** Certifications are a great way to validate your skills and make yourself more attractive to employers. Begin with entry-level certifications like CompTIA Security+ and work your way up to more advanced credentials as you gain experience.

- **Gain Practical Experience:** Hands-on experience is invaluable in cybersecurity. Seek out opportunities for internships, volunteer work, or personal projects that allow you to apply your skills in real-world scenarios.
- **Network with Professionals:** Networking is critical in cybersecurity. Join professional organisations, attend conferences, and connect with experienced professionals who can offer guidance and open doors to job opportunities.
- **Stay Informed:** The cybersecurity landscape is constantly evolving. Stay current by reading industry publications, participating in online forums, and following cybersecurity news and trends.
- **Consider a Degree:** While not always necessary, a degree in cybersecurity or a related field can provide a strong foundation and enhance your credentials, especially for those aiming for more technical or leadership roles.

Advancing Your Cybersecurity Career

Once you've established yourself in the cybersecurity field, advancing your career requires a combination of continuous learning, skill development, and strategic career planning. Here are some strategies to help you progress in your cybersecurity career:

Advancing Your Career

- **Pursue Advanced Certifications:** As you gain experience, consider pursuing advanced certifications that align with your career goals. These certifications can open doors to higher-level positions and demonstrate your expertise to employers.
- **Develop Leadership Skills:** If you're aiming for management or leadership roles, focus on developing skills in team management, strategic planning, and communication. Effective leaders are crucial in aligning security initiatives with business goals.
- **Specialise in a Niche Area:** Specialising in areas like cloud security, incident response, or threat intelligence can make you an expert in your field and increase your value to employers.

- **Stay Adaptive and Informed:** Continuously updating your skills and knowledge is essential in a field as dynamic as cybersecurity. Keeping pace with new threats and technological advancements will keep you competitive.
- **Seek Mentorship:** Mentorship can provide valuable guidance, support, and insight as you navigate your career. A mentor can help you identify opportunities for growth and development.
- **Consider Further Education:** For those aiming for executive roles, further education, such as an MBA or a specialised master's degree in cybersecurity, can enhance your strategic thinking and business acumen.

Conclusion

A career in cybersecurity offers numerous opportunities for growth, advancement, and impact. By building a strong foundation, gaining practical experience, and continuously learning, you can position yourself for success in this dynamic and rewarding field. As the demand for cybersecurity professionals continues to grow, those who are prepared and proactive will be well-equipped to seize the opportunities that lie ahead.

In the next chapter, we'll explore emerging threats and future trends in enterprise security, helping you stay ahead of the curve and prepare for the challenges of tomorrow.

17

Emerging Threats and Future Trends in Enterprise Security

Introduction to Emerging Threats and Future Trends

Cybersecurity is a battlefield that is constantly changing and evolving, driven by the rapid pace of technological advancement and the increasing sophistication of cybercriminals and threat actors. As organisations around the world embrace digital transformation, they face a growing array of threats that challenge their security postures and resilience. These threats are not static; they adapt and mutate, exploiting new technologies, vulnerabilities, and human behaviours.

In this chapter, we delve into the most pressing emerging threats that are reshaping the cybersecurity landscape, such as the evolution of ransomware, supply chain vulnerabilities, and Advanced Persistent Threats (APTs). We also explore future trends in enterprise security, including the adoption of zero trust architecture, the integration of Artificial Intelligence (AI) and machine learning in cybersecurity, the complexities of cloud and IoT security, and the increasing regulatory pressures that organisations must navigate. By understanding these threats and trends, organisations can develop a forward-thinking approach to cybersecurity, ensuring their defences are robust and adaptable in the face of ever-changing challenges.

Emerging Threats in Cybersecurity

The modern threat landscape is characterised by its complexity and the rapid evolution of attack methodologies. Cyber adversaries, ranging from individual hackers to nation-state actors, are continually

DOI: 10.1201/9781003585923-17

refining their tactics to bypass traditional defences and exploit emerging vulnerabilities.

Ransomware Evolution

Ransomware has evolved from a relatively simple form of malware to a sophisticated and multifaceted threat that targets organisations across all sectors. The impact of ransomware attacks is profound, with organisations facing not only financial losses but also reputational damage, operational disruption, and legal consequences.

- **Ransomware-as-a-Service (RaaS):** The rise of RaaS has transformed the ransomware landscape, making it accessible to a broader range of cybercriminals. RaaS platforms operate much like legitimate software services, offering ransomware kits for sale or rent, along with customer support and payment processing. This commercialisation has led to a surge in ransomware attacks, as even those with minimal technical skills can now launch sophisticated campaigns.
- **Double and Triple Extortion:** Modern ransomware attacks have moved beyond merely encrypting data. In double extortion schemes, attackers exfiltrate sensitive data before encrypting it, threatening to release the data publicly if the ransom is not paid. Triple extortion adds another layer of pressure by targeting an organisation's partners, suppliers, or customers, demanding ransoms from them as well.
- **Targeting Critical Infrastructure:** The targeting of critical infrastructure by ransomware groups represents a significant escalation in the threat landscape. Attacks on sectors such as healthcare, energy, and transportation not only disrupt operations but can also endanger lives. The Colonial Pipeline and Irish Health Service attacks are stark reminders of the potential for catastrophic consequences.
- **Evolving Ransom Payment Models:** As governments and law enforcement agencies crack down on ransomware payments, attackers are adapting their strategies. Some ransomware groups are now offering 'discounts' for quick payment or threatening to increase the ransom over time. Others are

experimenting with new payment methods, such as crypto-currencies designed for enhanced privacy.

Supply Chain Vulnerabilities

Supply chain attacks have emerged as a critical threat, exploiting the interconnected nature of modern business operations. These attacks can be particularly insidious because they target the trust relationships between organisations and their suppliers, partners, and service providers. Figure 17.1 shows the risks and mitigations of protecting a simplified supply chain.

- **Third-Party and Fourth-Party Risks:** Organisations increasingly depend on third-party vendors for critical services, including software development, cloud hosting, and IT management. However, the security of these vendors is often beyond the direct control of the hiring organisation.

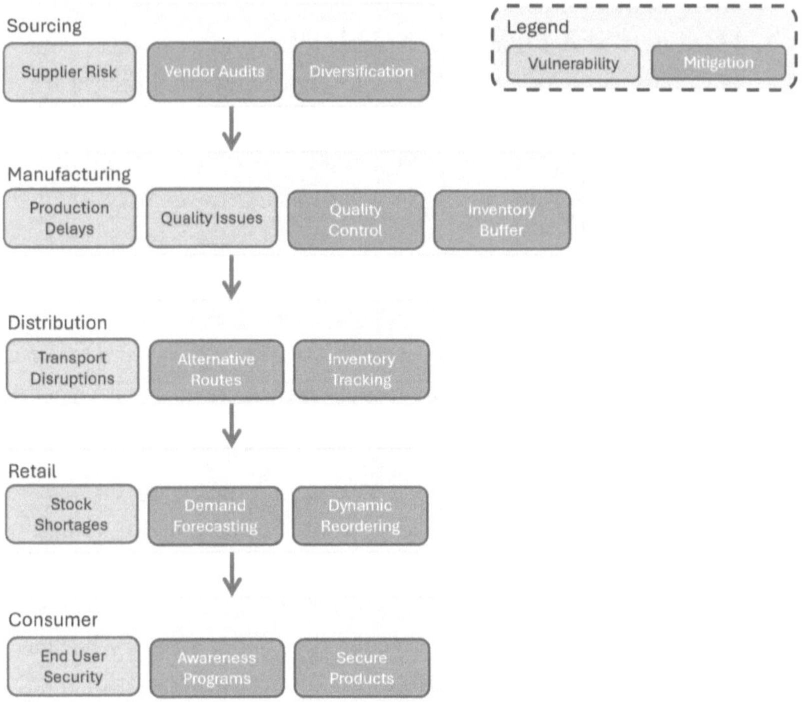

Figure 17.1 Supply chain stages with aligned key vulnerabilities and corresponding mitigation strategies.

Fourth-party risks arise when these vendors, in turn, rely on their own suppliers, creating a complex web of dependencies that can be difficult to secure.

- **Software Supply Chain Attacks:** In a software supply chain attack, attackers infiltrate the development or distribution process of a software provider, inserting malicious code into legitimate software updates or applications. When these compromised updates are deployed across the customer base, the malware spreads quickly and efficiently, often evading traditional security measures.
- **Managed Service Providers (MSPs):** MSPs are prime targets for cybercriminals because they manage IT systems for multiple clients. A successful attack on an MSP can give attackers access to a vast number of organisations, multiplying the potential impact of the breach. The 2021 Kaseya VSA attack, where ransomware was deployed through a compromised MSP, exemplifies the severe risks posed by supply chain vulnerabilities.
- **Hardware and Firmware Attacks:** Beyond software, supply chain attacks can also target hardware and firmware. Compromised hardware components or tampered firmware can introduce backdoors or vulnerabilities that are difficult to detect and mitigate, posing long-term risks to security.

Advanced Persistent Threats (APTs)

APTs represent some of the most sophisticated cyber threats, often orchestrated by well-funded and highly skilled groups with specific strategic objectives. These attacks are typically characterised by their persistence, stealth, and tailored tactics.

- **Long-Term Infiltration:** APTs are designed to remain undetected within a network for extended periods, sometimes months or even years. This long-term access allows attackers to carefully plan and execute their operations, whether it's stealing sensitive information, disrupting operations, or manipulating data.

- **Customised and Evolving Tactics:** APT groups invest significant resources in reconnaissance and customisation. They study their targets in detail, adapting their tactics to exploit specific vulnerabilities within the target's infrastructure. This makes APTs particularly difficult to defend against, as they often bypass traditional security measures.
- **Nation-State Sponsorship:** Many APTs are believed to be sponsored or directly executed by nation-states, often targeting critical infrastructure, government agencies, and key industries. These attacks are usually motivated by geopolitical objectives, such as espionage, economic disruption, or military advantage.
- **Supply Chain Infiltration:** APTs increasingly exploit supply chain vulnerabilities to gain access to their primary targets. By compromising a trusted vendor or service provider, attackers can bypass direct defences and establish a foothold within the target organisation.

Insider Threats

Insider threats are among the most challenging to detect and mitigate because they originate from within the organisation. Insiders have legitimate access to systems and data, making their actions harder to distinguish from normal activity.

- **Malicious Insiders:** Malicious insiders are individuals who intentionally abuse their access for personal gain, to cause harm, or to assist external attackers. These insiders may be motivated by financial incentives, ideological beliefs, or a desire for revenge against their employer.
- **Negligent Insiders:** Negligent insiders are well-meaning employees who inadvertently cause security breaches through careless or uninformed actions. This can include falling victim to phishing attacks, misconfiguring systems, or mishandling sensitive information.
- **Compromised Insiders:** Compromised insiders are individuals who are coerced, blackmailed, or manipulated into aiding attackers. These insiders may not even be aware of the full extent of the damage they are enabling, making it difficult to identify and stop their activities.

- **Hybrid Threats:** Some insiders may fall into more than one category, such as a negligent insider who becomes compromised after falling for a phishing attack. These hybrid threats further complicate the detection and mitigation of insider risks.

AI-Powered Attacks

The integration of AI into cyberattacks is transforming the threat landscape, making attacks more adaptive, scalable, and difficult to counter. AI enables attackers to automate and enhance various stages of their operations, from reconnaissance to execution.

- **AI-Driven Social Engineering:** AI can be used to craft highly convincing phishing emails, voice messages, or deepfake videos that are tailored to specific targets. By analysing publicly available data, AI systems can create personalised messages that are more likely to deceive victims.
- **Autonomous Malware:** AI-enhanced malware can autonomously adapt its tactics based on the environment it encounters. For example, it might change its behaviour to avoid detection by security tools, or it might choose different propagation methods based on the network topology.
- **Deepfake Technology:** Deepfake technology, which uses AI to generate realistic but fake audio, video, or images, poses a significant threat to security. Deepfakes can be used to impersonate executives, manipulate public opinion, or bypass biometric security systems.
- **AI-Augmented Ransomware:** AI can enhance ransomware by enabling it to identify and target high-value files, adjust ransom demands based on the victim's financial resources, or spread more efficiently across networks.

Future Trends in Enterprise Security

As the threat landscape continues to evolve, so too must the strategies and technologies that organisations employ to defend themselves. The following trends are expected to shape the future of enterprise security, influencing how organisations design, implement, and manage their cybersecurity defences.

Zero Trust Architecture

The zero- trust model represents a significant shift from traditional perimeter-based security approaches. In a zero trust environment, no entity, whether inside or outside the network, is inherently trusted. Instead, continuous verification and strict access controls are applied to every user, device, and connection.

- **Continuous Verification:** Zero trust requires continuous verification of identities, devices, and access requests. This involves using Multi-Factor Authentication (MFA), endpoint security checks, and behavioural analytics to ensure that only legitimate users and devices can access resources.
- **Least Privilege Access:** The principle of least privilege is central to zero trust, ensuring that users and devices are granted only the minimum level of access necessary to perform their tasks. This limits the potential damage that can be caused by compromised accounts or insider threats.
- **Micro-Segmentation:** Zero trust environments use micro-segmentation to divide the network into smaller, isolated zones, each with its own security controls. This prevents attackers from moving laterally within the network if they manage to breach one segment.
- **Dynamic Access Control:** Access decisions in a zero trust architecture are dynamic and context-aware, taking into account factors such as the user's location, device status, and the sensitivity of the requested resource. This allows organisations to adapt their security posture in real time based on changing conditions.

AI and Machine Learning in Defence

Just as attackers are leveraging AI to enhance their operations, defenders are increasingly using AI and machine learning to strengthen their security defences. These technologies enable more effective threat detection, faster response times, and improved overall security resilience.

- **AI-Powered Threat Detection:** AI and machine learning algorithms can analyse vast amounts of security data in real time, identifying patterns and anomalies that may indicate a threat. These systems can detect new and unknown threats by learning from previous incidents and adapting their detection criteria accordingly.
- **Behavioural Analytics:** AI can be used to monitor and analyse user behaviour, detecting deviations from normal patterns that may suggest a compromised account or insider threat. This proactive approach helps identify threats before they can cause significant damage.
- **Automated Incident Response:** AI can automate the initial stages of incident response, such as isolating affected systems, blocking malicious IP addresses, and generating incident reports. This reduces the time it takes to respond to threats and allows human analysts to focus on more complex tasks.
- **Predictive Analytics:** AI-driven predictive analytics can help organisations anticipate future threats by analysing trends and historical data. This enables security teams to take pre-emptive action, such as patching vulnerabilities or adjusting security policies, before an attack occurs.

Cloud and Multi-Cloud Security

As more organisations migrate their operations to the cloud, securing these environments has become a top priority. The adoption of multi-cloud strategies, where organisations use multiple cloud service providers, adds further complexity to cloud security management.

- **Cloud Security Posture Management (CSPM):** CSPM tools help organisations manage and secure their cloud environments by continuously monitoring for misconfigurations, vulnerabilities, and compliance issues. These tools provide visibility into cloud resources and help ensure that security policies are consistently applied across all cloud environments.

- **Identity and Access Management (IAM):** Effective IAM is critical for securing cloud environments, particularly in multi-cloud scenarios. Organisations must implement robust IAM policies that enforce multi-factor authentication, role-based access control, and continuous monitoring of user activity.
- **Serverless and Container Security:** As organisations adopt serverless computing and containerised applications, securing these environments has become increasingly important. Security measures must be integrated into the development and deployment processes to protect against vulnerabilities and misconfigurations.
- **Data Encryption and Privacy:** With sensitive data increasingly being stored and processed in the cloud, ensuring robust encryption and privacy measures is essential. Organisations must implement encryption both in transit and at rest and ensure that their cloud providers comply with data protection regulations.

Internet of Things (IoT) Security

The proliferation of IoT devices across industries presents new security challenges. These devices often lack robust security features, making them attractive targets for attackers looking to gain access to networks or disrupt operations.

- **Device Management and Security:** Effective IoT security requires robust device management, including regular updates, patching, and monitoring of device behaviour. Organisations must also implement network segmentation and access controls to limit the impact of compromised devices.
- **Standardisation and Regulation:** The lack of standardisation in IoT security complicates efforts to implement consistent security measures across diverse devices and platforms. As the IoT ecosystem grows, there is a need for industry-wide standards and regulations to ensure that devices are secure by design.
- **Industrial IoT (IIoT) Security:** Securing IIoT devices, which are used in critical infrastructure sectors like manufacturing,

energy, and transportation, is essential to protect against attacks that could disrupt operations or cause physical damage. This requires specialised security measures, including real-time monitoring, anomaly detection, and secure communication protocols.

- **IoT Threat Intelligence:** As IoT devices become more prevalent, there is a growing need for threat intelligence focused on IoT-specific threats. Organisations must stay informed about the latest vulnerabilities and attack methods targeting IoT devices and adapt their security strategies accordingly.

Regulatory and Compliance Challenges

The regulatory landscape for cybersecurity is becoming increasingly complex, with new laws and standards being introduced at a rapid pace. Organisations must navigate these challenges while ensuring that their security practices remain effective and compliant.

- **Data Privacy Regulations:** Regulations such as the General Data Protection Regulation (GDPR) in Europe and the California Consumer Privacy Act (CCPA) in the United States impose strict requirements on how organisations handle personal data. Compliance requires robust data protection measures, transparent data processing practices, and the ability to respond quickly to data breaches.
- **Cybersecurity Maturity Models:** Models like the Cybersecurity Maturity Model Certification (CMMC) for defence contractors require organisations to demonstrate their cybersecurity capabilities and adherence to specific security practices. Achieving and maintaining compliance involves implementing detailed controls, conducting regular audits, and continuously improving security practices.
- **Cross-border Data Transfers:** The complexity of cross-border data transfers, particularly in the light of regulations like GDPR, presents challenges for global organisations. Ensuring compliance across different jurisdictions requires careful planning, robust data protection strategies, and the ability to adapt to varying regulatory requirements.

- **Evolving Regulatory Landscape:** The regulatory landscape is continually evolving, with new laws and standards being introduced in response to emerging threats. Organisations must stay informed about these changes and be prepared to adjust their security practices to remain compliant.

Preparing for the Future of Enterprise Security

To navigate the evolving cybersecurity landscape effectively, organisations must adopt a proactive and adaptive approach. This involves continuously assessing and updating security strategies, investing in advanced technologies, and fostering a culture of security awareness and resilience.

Proactive Security Posture

Adopting a proactive security posture means anticipating and addressing threats before they can cause significant harm. This involves implementing advanced threat detection and response capabilities, conducting regular threat hunting, and staying ahead of emerging threats.

- **Advanced Threat Detection:** Invest in AI-powered threat detection tools that can analyse vast amounts of data in real time, identifying patterns and anomalies that may indicate a threat. These tools can detect new and unknown threats by learning from previous incidents and adapting their detection criteria accordingly.
- **Regular Threat Hunting:** Conduct regular threat hunting exercises to identify and address potential threats before they can escalate. This proactive approach helps organisations stay ahead of attackers and reduce the risk of successful breaches.
- **Pre-emptive Security Measures:** Implement pre-emptive security measures, such as patching vulnerabilities, adjusting security policies, and deploying new security technologies, to address potential threats before they can be exploited.

Investment in Training and Awareness

Ensuring that employees at all levels are trained in cybersecurity best practices and are aware of emerging threats is essential for building a resilient security culture. Regular training and simulations help reinforce security awareness and prepare employees to respond effectively to incidents.

- **Regular Security Training:** Provide ongoing security training for all employees, covering topics such as phishing, social engineering, and data protection. Training should be tailored to the specific roles and responsibilities of employees to ensure that they understand the risks and how to mitigate them.
- **Phishing Simulations:** Conduct regular phishing simulations to test employees' ability to recognise and respond to phishing attacks. These simulations help identify areas for improvement and reinforce the importance of vigilance.
- **Security Awareness Campaigns:** Launch security awareness campaigns that promote key security messages and provide employees with practical tips for staying secure. These campaigns should be ongoing and integrated into the organisation's overall culture.

Leveraging Advanced Technologies

Investing in advanced security technologies, such as AI, machine learning, and zero trust architecture, is essential for enhancing an organisation's ability to detect, respond to, and mitigate threats. These technologies provide the tools and capabilities needed to stay ahead of attackers in an increasingly complex threat landscape.

- **AI and Machine Learning:** Leverage AI and machine learning to enhance threat detection, automate incident response, and improve overall security resilience. These technologies enable organisations to analyse vast amounts of data in real time, identify patterns and anomalies, and respond to threats more quickly and effectively.
- **Zero Trust Architecture:** Implement a zero trust architecture that enforces strict access controls, continuous verification,

and micro-segmentation. This approach reduces the risk of insider threats and lateral movement by attackers, ensuring that only legitimate users and devices can access resources.
- **Cloud Security Solutions:** Invest in cloud security solutions, such as Cloud Security Posture Management (CSPM) tools and Identity and Access Management (IAM) systems, to secure cloud environments and ensure compliance with regulations.

Industry Collaboration

Engaging in industry collaboration and information sharing is critical for staying informed about the latest threats, vulnerabilities, and best practices. Participating in industry groups and threat intelligence networks can provide valuable insights and resources for improving security.

- **Threat Intelligence Sharing:** Join industry-specific Information Sharing and Analysis Centres (ISACs) to receive timely threat intelligence, share experiences, and collaborate on improving security across the sector.
- **Collaboration with Partners:** Collaborate with partners, suppliers, and service providers to ensure that security practices are aligned and that vulnerabilities in the supply chain are addressed.
- **Participation in Industry Forums:** Participate in industry forums and conferences to stay informed about emerging threats, new technologies, and best practices. These events provide opportunities to learn from peers, share experiences, and build valuable connections.

Regulatory Compliance

Staying informed about evolving regulatory requirements and ensuring that your organisation's security practices align with current and future regulations is essential for maintaining compliance and avoiding penalties.

- **Compliance Monitoring:** Implement compliance monitoring and reporting tools to track regulatory changes, automate reporting, and ensure adherence to data protection laws in all regions where the organisation operates.
- **Adaptation to Regulatory Changes:** Stay informed about evolving regulatory requirements and be prepared to adjust security practices to remain compliant. This may involve implementing new controls, conducting additional audits, or updating policies and procedures.
- **Cross-Border Data Protection:** Develop robust data protection strategies for managing cross-border data transfers, ensuring compliance with varying regulations in different jurisdictions. This may involve implementing data localisation measures, encryption, and secure data transfer agreements.

Conclusion

The cybersecurity landscape is in a constant state of flux, with new threats and challenges emerging at an unprecedented pace. To protect themselves against these threats, organisations must adopt a forward-looking approach to security, leveraging advanced technologies, proactive strategies, and continuous adaptation.

By understanding and preparing for the emerging threats and future trends outlined in this chapter, organisations can build a more resilient security posture, ensuring that they are well-equipped to face the challenges of tomorrow. As we move into the future, the key to successful enterprise security will be the ability to anticipate, adapt, and evolve in response to an ever-changing threat landscape.

In the next chapter, we will explore how to integrate security into the software development lifecycle, focusing on best practices for secure coding, threat modelling, and vulnerability management.

18
Developing and Implementing a Cybersecurity Strategy

Introduction to Cybersecurity Strategy

Cybersecurity is no longer just a technical issue; it has become a strategic imperative. As organisations increasingly rely on digital systems to manage critical aspects of their operations, everything from handling customer data to coordinating supply chains, they become more vulnerable to cyber threats. These threats can take many forms, from ransomware attacks to insider breaches, and they have the potential to severely damage an organisation's operations, finances, and reputation.

Developing a comprehensive cybersecurity strategy is essential for any organisation that wants to protect its assets, maintain the trust of customers, comply with regulatory requirements, and ensure its long-term success. However, it's not just about throwing technology at the problem. A good cybersecurity strategy must be carefully crafted to fit the unique needs and risks of the organisation. This requires a deep understanding of the company's business objectives, its risk profile, and its resources.

A cybersecurity strategy serves as the blueprint for how an organisation will protect itself from cyber threats, respond to incidents, and stay compliant with relevant regulations. Importantly, the strategy should align with broader organisational goals, ensuring that security supports the business rather than hindering it. Security needs to be seen as an enabler, not an obstacle.

This chapter will explore the essential components of a cybersecurity strategy, including risk assessment, setting strategic goals, implementing security controls, incident response planning, and

DOI: 10.1201/9781003585923-18

continuous monitoring. We will also look at how to align cybersecurity efforts with business objectives to create a flexible and robust security framework.

The Importance of a Cybersecurity Strategy

A well-defined cybersecurity strategy is the cornerstone of an organisation's ability to manage risks and protect itself from a range of threats. In an environment where data breaches and cyberattacks are becoming increasingly frequent and costly, businesses that operate without a strategic approach to security are setting themselves up for failure. The consequences of poor cybersecurity planning can range from severe financial losses and operational disruptions to regulatory penalties and reputational damage that may take years to repair.

Key Benefits of a Cybersecurity Strategy

1. **Risk Management:** A structured strategy enables an organisation to systematically identify, assess, and mitigate risks. By understanding its unique vulnerabilities and threats, an organisation can make informed decisions about where to focus its security resources, ensuring the most critical areas are protected.
2. **Alignment with Business Goals:** A cybersecurity strategy ensures that security measures align with the broader business objectives of the organisation. Security should not act as a barrier to growth or innovation, but rather as a support system that enables the organisation to achieve its goals safely and securely. When security is integrated into business processes, it garners executive support and becomes a priority for everyone within the organisation.
3. **Regulatory Compliance:** As regulatory frameworks around data protection and cybersecurity become more complex, having a cybersecurity strategy in place is crucial for maintaining compliance with relevant laws and standards. A good strategy helps avoid legal penalties, ensures that stakeholders' security expectations are met, and demonstrates the organisation's commitment to safeguarding sensitive information.

4. **Incident Response and Resilience:** An effective cybersecurity strategy includes detailed plans for responding to security incidents. These plans ensure that the organisation can respond quickly and effectively to mitigate the damage from a breach, restore normal operations, and reduce the long-term impact of the incident. Resilience is key; the ability to recover and continue operating after an attack can make the difference between a temporary setback and a catastrophic failure.
5. **Continuous Improvement:** The cybersecurity landscape is constantly evolving, with new threats emerging all the time. A robust cybersecurity strategy provides a framework for continuous monitoring and improvement, allowing an organisation to stay ahead of potential threats by regularly reviewing and updating its security measures.

Key Components of a Cybersecurity Strategy

Developing a strong cybersecurity strategy involves several critical steps, each designed to provide a comprehensive and dynamic approach to protecting the organisation's assets and operations. Below are the main components that every cybersecurity strategy should include.

Risk Assessment

The first step in any cybersecurity strategy is conducting a thorough risk assessment. This process involves identifying the risks the organisation faces, assessing the likelihood of those risks materialising, and understanding the potential impact on the organisation if they do occur. By evaluating these factors, the organisation can prioritise its security efforts and focus on mitigating the most significant risks.

Steps for Conducting a Risk Assessment

- **Identify Assets:** The organisation must determine what assets need protection. This includes sensitive data, critical systems, intellectual property, and anything else that, if compromised, would disrupt operations or cause financial loss.

- **Identify Threats:** The next step is to identify the potential threats to those assets. These could range from cybercriminals and malware to insider threats and natural disasters.
- **Assess Vulnerabilities:** Once the threats have been identified, the organisation must assess its vulnerabilities. Vulnerabilities are weaknesses that could be exploited by threats, such as outdated software, insufficient access controls, or untrained staff.
- **Determine Impact and Likelihood:** For each risk, the organisation should determine how likely it is to occur and what the potential impact would be. This helps prioritise the risks that need immediate attention.
- **Develop a Risk Mitigation Plan:** Based on the assessment, the organisation can develop a plan to mitigate the identified risks. This plan should include specific actions and security measures to reduce the likelihood and impact of each risk.

Goal Setting

After assessing the risks, the organisation should establish clear cybersecurity goals. These goals should be aligned with the broader objectives of the organisation and serve as a roadmap for implementing security measures. Goals should be specific, measurable, and achievable within a reasonable timeframe.

Steps for Setting Cybersecurity Goals

- **Define Strategic Objectives:** The organisation should begin by defining its high-level cybersecurity objectives. These objectives provide direction and ensure that the organisation's cybersecurity efforts are aligned with its mission and long-term goals.
- **Set Specific, Measurable Goals:** Once the strategic objectives are defined, they should be broken down into specific, measurable goals. These goals might include reducing the time it takes to detect and respond to incidents, improving the security of critical systems, or increasing employee awareness of cybersecurity best practices.
- **Align Goals with Business Priorities:** Cybersecurity goals should always support the organisation's business priorities.

For example, if the organisation is focusing on digital transformation, its cybersecurity goals should ensure that new technologies and platforms are securely integrated.

- **Communicate Goals across the Organisation:** It's important that everyone in the organisation understands the cybersecurity goals and their role in achieving them. This includes executive leadership, IT teams, and business units.

Security Controls

Once the goals are in place, the next step is to implement security controls. Security controls are the tools, processes, and policies that the organisation will use to protect its assets and reduce the risks identified during the assessment.

Types of Security Controls

- **Preventive Controls:** These controls are designed to prevent security incidents from occurring. They include firewalls, encryption, and multi-factor authentication.
- **Detective Controls:** These controls help identify security incidents as they occur. Examples include intrusion Detection Systems (IDS), monitoring tools, and logging systems.
- **Corrective Controls:** Corrective controls are used to mitigate the impact of a security incident once it has occurred. These might include incident response procedures, data recovery processes, and system restoration techniques.
- **Deterrent Controls:** These measures are intended to discourage potential attackers from attempting to breach the organisation's systems. Deterrent controls might include strict access controls, visible security policies, and regular training programmes for employees.

Incident Response Planning

An effective cybersecurity strategy includes a comprehensive incident response plan that outlines how the organisation will respond to security incidents. The plan should cover both immediate and long-term actions to contain and recover from an attack, as well as measures to prevent future incidents.

Key Elements of an Incident Response Plan

- **Preparation:** Ensure that the organisation has the tools, resources, and policies in place to respond to incidents. This includes forming an incident response team and defining roles and responsibilities.
- **Identification:** Develop processes for detecting and identifying security incidents in real time.
- **Containment:** Establish procedures to isolate affected systems and prevent the spread of malicious activity.
- **Eradication:** Remove the root cause of the incident and eliminate any remaining threats.
- **Recovery:** Restore systems to normal operation, ensuring that data is recovered, and vulnerabilities are addressed.
- **Lessons Learned:** After an incident, review what went wrong and what worked well. This feedback should be used to improve future responses.

Continuous Monitoring and Improvement

Cybersecurity is not a one-time effort but an ongoing process. Continuous monitoring and improvement are essential for maintaining the effectiveness of the cybersecurity strategy over time. As new threats emerge and the organisation evolves, its security measures must be regularly reviewed and updated.

Steps for Continuous Monitoring and Improvement

- **Implement Continuous Monitoring:** Use security tools and processes to continuously monitor systems for signs of potential threats or vulnerabilities.
- **Conduct Regular Security Audits:** Periodically audit the organisation's security measures to ensure they are still effective and aligned with the overall strategy.
- **Update Security Policies:** Revise and update security policies as the organisation's needs change and as new threats emerge.

- **Invest in Employee Training:** Regularly update training programmes to reflect new threats and ensure that all employees are aware of cybersecurity best practices.
- **Foster a Culture of Continuous Improvement:** Encourage a mindset of ongoing learning and improvement within the organisation, ensuring that cybersecurity is seen as an evolving process.

Aligning Cybersecurity with Business Objectives

A successful cybersecurity strategy must be aligned with the organisation's overall business objectives. This alignment ensures that cybersecurity supports, rather than hinders, the organisation's growth, innovation, and operational efficiency. By integrating security into the business strategy, cybersecurity becomes a value driver rather than a cost centre.

Steps for Aligning Cybersecurity with Business Objectives

1. **Understand Business Priorities:** Start by gaining a clear understanding of the organisation's top priorities, whether it's growth, customer trust, or operational efficiency.
2. **Engage with Stakeholders:** Engage key stakeholders across the organisation to ensure that their needs and concerns are considered when developing the cybersecurity strategy.
3. **Align Security Goals with Business Goals:** Ensure that the goals of the cybersecurity strategy are directly tied to the organisation's broader business objectives, helping to secure leadership support and integration into decision-making processes.
4. **Communicate the Value of Cybersecurity:** Clearly communicate the value of strong cybersecurity to stakeholders at all levels, emphasising how it protects the organisation's assets, reputation, and competitive advantage.
5. **Integrate Security into Decision-Making:** Involve security teams in strategic planning and decision-making processes across the organisation, ensuring that security is a consideration in every business decision.

6. **Monitor and Report on Progress:** Regularly track the performance of the cybersecurity strategy using KPIs and metrics, and report progress to executive leadership.

Conclusion

Developing and implementing a comprehensive cybersecurity strategy is no longer just a technical requirement, it's a business imperative that directly influences an organisation's ability to thrive. As we've discussed throughout this chapter, cybersecurity goes beyond simply installing firewalls or antivirus software. It demands a well-rounded, forward-thinking strategy that addresses not only today's threats but anticipates the challenges of tomorrow. Without a strategy in place, organisations are not only exposing themselves to potential financial and reputational damage but are also jeopardising their ability to innovate, grow, and maintain the trust of their customers.

A solid cybersecurity strategy isn't built in a day; it requires careful planning, collaboration across departments, and continuous improvement. It starts with a thorough risk assessment, which forms the foundation of informed decision-making. Knowing your organisation's vulnerabilities and the threats it faces allows for a more targeted and efficient allocation of resources. From there, setting clear and achievable goals aligned with business objectives ensures that cybersecurity doesn't operate in isolation but supports the organisation's growth and innovation. Security must be embedded in every level of the business, from IT to leadership, so that it becomes part of the company's DNA, rather than an afterthought or a box-ticking exercise.

Moreover, implementing robust security controls helps mitigate risks, but this is only one aspect of a successful strategy. A key differentiator between resilient organisations and those that struggle is how prepared they are to respond to incidents. Incidents will happen; it's not a matter of *if* but *when*. What matters is having a well-defined, rehearsed incident response plan in place that allows the organisation to contain threats quickly, minimise damage, and recover faster. Companies that prepare for these eventualities are not only more resilient in the face of cyberattacks but also better positioned to maintain business continuity and protect their reputation.

Continuous monitoring and improvement are also essential pillars of a cybersecurity strategy. Cyber threats evolve constantly, and an organisation's defences must evolve with them. The strategy you put in place today will need regular updates and adjustments as new threats emerge, technology advances, and business needs change. Organisations that commit to ongoing improvement will not only be better protected but will also be more adaptable and responsive to the shifting landscape. This flexibility can be a significant competitive advantage in industries where digital transformation is rapidly advancing, and agility is key.

A well-implemented cybersecurity strategy can also serve as a competitive differentiator. In today's market, customers, partners, and investors are increasingly prioritising security. Organisations that demonstrate a strong commitment to safeguarding data and ensuring operational resilience stand out in the marketplace. Customers want to know that their data is safe, and partners want to work with companies that are trustworthy. A cybersecurity strategy that prioritises these aspects can be a powerful tool for building stronger relationships with all stakeholders.

19
Conclusion and the Path Forward

Final Thoughts and Considerations

What a journey we've been on! From the first step of laying the groundwork for enterprise security to exploring cutting-edge technologies and strategic incident response, we've certainly covered a lot of ground. Cybersecurity today isn't just a 'nice to have', it's the bedrock of any organisation's success. The days of treating it like a separate, niche concern are long gone. Today, it's central to everything from safeguarding operations to building trust with customers, partners, and stakeholders.

Think about it, every topic we've explored, whether it's threat intelligence, security architecture, or automation, ultimately points to one thing: building a security posture that not only protects but also empowers your organisation. We're no longer just securing assets; we're enabling innovation, growth, and resilience in an unpredictable world.

But if there's one thing you take away from this book, let it be this: cybersecurity isn't static. It's a constantly shifting landscape. That's what makes it so challenging, and so rewarding. The threats evolve, so our defences and strategies must too. It's about being proactive, not reactive. Security shouldn't be an afterthought; it needs to be baked into every decision, every process, and every level of your organisation. It's no longer about ticking boxes – security needs to be woven into the DNA of your business.

DOI: 10.1201/9781003585923-19

The Importance of a Holistic Approach

Throughout this book, we've stressed the value of a holistic approach to cybersecurity. It's not enough to just invest in the latest tech, although that's certainly important. It's about the bigger picture: aligning your security efforts with your business goals, fostering a culture where everyone understands their role in protecting the organisation, and keeping pace with the ever-changing threat landscape. This approach builds a security framework that's not only strong but also adaptable to future challenges.

Key Strategic Takeaways

Let's quickly recap the key takeaways that can guide your security efforts moving forward:

1. **Cybersecurity as a Strategic Imperative:** Cybersecurity is no longer just about protecting your organisation's assets. It's integral to your overall business strategy. By embedding security into your strategic planning, you're enabling innovation, maintaining trust, and supporting sustainable growth.
2. **Risk Management as the Foundation:** Everything starts with risk. By understanding, assessing, and prioritising risks, you can allocate your resources more effectively. Focus on addressing your most critical vulnerabilities first, this is the foundation of a solid security strategy.
3. **Continuous Improvement and Adaptation:** Cybersecurity is never 'done'. The threat landscape is always shifting, so you need to keep evolving. Regularly review and update your security measures to stay ahead of new threats and ensure your defences remain effective.
4. **Cultivating a Security-Aware Culture:** People are often the weakest link in any security strategy, but they can also be your greatest asset. Invest in creating a culture where everyone – from the C-suite to entry-level employees, understands the importance of cybersecurity and their role in protecting the organisation.

5. **Incident Response Preparedness:** No matter how robust your security, incidents will happen. What sets successful organisations apart is their ability to respond quickly and efficiently. Having a solid, well-tested incident response plan can drastically minimise the damage of an attack and keep your business running smoothly.
6. **Leveraging Emerging Technologies:** AI, machine learning, automation, these are more than just buzzwords. They're powerful tools that can help you improve everything from threat detection to response times. Embracing emerging tech can give you a crucial edge.
7. **Alignment with Business Objectives:** Cybersecurity shouldn't be a roadblock to innovation. Instead, it should be aligned with your business goals, helping you achieve your objectives while keeping risks in check. Whether it's protecting intellectual property or supporting digital transformation, security should enable, not stifle, your organisation.
8. **Long-Term Resilience:** Building resilience goes beyond preventing attacks, it's about ensuring your organisation can bounce back quickly when incidents occur. This means having strong recovery plans, redundancy in your systems, and clear communication strategies in place.

The Path Forward

So, where do you go from here? What's the path forward in an increasingly complex cybersecurity landscape? Let's break it down into some actionable steps that can guide your journey:

1. **Assess and Reassess:** Regularly evaluate your cybersecurity posture. This isn't a 'set it and forget it' task. You need to constantly look for weaknesses and areas for improvement. Stay agile and evolve your strategies to match the current threat landscape.

2. **Invest in Talent and Training:** Technology alone won't solve your problems. The human element is critical. Invest in your people, giving them the training they need to stay on top of the latest threats and security practices. Encourage continuous learning and make security awareness part of your organisation's DNA.
3. **Innovate and Adapt:** Stay ahead of the curve by embracing innovation. Whether it's adopting zero trust architecture, improving cloud security, or implementing AI-driven threat detection, don't be afraid to experiment and adapt. What worked yesterday may not work tomorrow.
4. **Collaborate and Share Knowledge:** Cybersecurity is a team sport. Collaborate with peers, participate in information-sharing networks, and stay engaged with the broader cybersecurity community. The more we share knowledge, the better protected we all are.
5. **Prepare for the Unexpected:** Threats are unpredictable, but your response doesn't have to be. Develop and regularly test your incident response and disaster recovery plans. Make sure your organisation can keep running, even in the face of an attack.
6. **Engage Leadership:** Cybersecurity needs to be a priority from the top down. Engage your executive leadership in regular discussions about security and make sure they understand its importance. Their support is critical for securing ongoing investment and fostering a culture of security.
7. **Commit to Continuous Improvement:** This is an ongoing journey. Cybersecurity doesn't have an end point. Commit to continuous improvement in every aspect of your security strategy, whether it's risk management, technology, or training. Keep learning, keep adapting.

Final Words

At the end of the day, cybersecurity is about more than just preventing attacks. It's about building resilience, protecting what matters most, and enabling your business to thrive in the digital age. The strategies, tools, and insights we've discussed in this book provide a strong foundation but remember, this isn't the end of the road. The work of securing your organisation is never truly finished.

Yes, the challenges are significant. Cybersecurity is complex, and the stakes are high. But with a proactive, strategic approach, you can navigate these challenges, protect your organisation, and emerge stronger and more secure. This isn't just about defence; it's about positioning your organisation to grow and succeed in a world that's becoming increasingly digital.

Looking Beyond: The Future of Cybersecurity

While this book has covered the essentials of enterprise security, the field of cybersecurity continues to evolve at lightning speed. As you move forward, here are some advanced areas worth exploring that could shape the future of cybersecurity:

- **Advanced Threat Hunting:** Take your threat detection to the next level by diving into proactive threat-hunting techniques. AI and machine learning will play an ever-increasing role in helping you anticipate and neutralise threats before they become full-blown incidents.

Cloud and IoT Security: With more organisations adopting cloud services and integrating IoT devices into their operations, the security challenges in these areas are becoming more complex. Gaining expertise here will be critical for staying ahead of the curve.

Cybersecurity Leadership: As cybersecurity becomes more strategic, leadership skills will become increasingly important. Understanding how to manage cybersecurity at the executive level will be crucial for those aspiring to senior roles.

- **Global Cybersecurity Trends:** Cybersecurity is a global issue, with international regulations and sophisticated, cross-border threats. Stay informed about global trends, regulations, and emerging standards to ensure your organisation remains compliant and prepared for international challenges.

By expanding your knowledge in these areas, you'll not only keep your organisation secure but also ensure you're ready to tackle the future of cybersecurity head-on.

Appendix A

Glossary of Terms

A

- **Access Control:** Mechanisms and policies that restrict access to systems, networks, or data, ensuring only authorised users can interact with specific resources.
- **Advanced Persistent Threat (APT):** A prolonged and targeted cyberattack in which an intruder gains access to a network and remains undetected for an extended period.
- **Artificial Intelligence (AI) in Cybersecurity:** The use of AI technologies to enhance cybersecurity measures, such as automated threat detection and response.
- **Attack Surface:** The total number of points or vectors through which an unauthorised user can try to enter data into or extract data from an environment.
- **Authentication:** The process of verifying the identity of a user, device, or system, often as a prerequisite for gaining access to resources.

B

- **Behavioural Analytics:** The process of analysing user behaviour patterns to detect deviations that may indicate security threats such as compromised accounts.
- **Botnet:** A network of private computers infected with malicious software and controlled as a group without the owners' knowledge, often used to launch DDoS attacks.
- **Business Continuity Planning (BCP):** The process of creating systems of prevention and recovery to deal with potential threats to an organisation, ensuring that operations can continue during and after a disaster.

C

- **Cloud Security:** A set of policies, controls, procedures, and technologies that work together to protect cloud-based systems, data, and infrastructure.
- **Credential Stuffing:** A type of cyberattack where stolen account credentials are used to gain unauthorised access to user accounts.
- **Cross-Site Scripting (XSS):** A vulnerability that allows attackers to inject malicious scripts into web pages viewed by other users.
- **Cyber Hygiene:** The practices and steps that users and organisations take to maintain system health and improve online security, such as regular software updates, using strong passwords, and securing hardware.
- **Cybersecurity Incident Response:** The process of detecting, responding to, and recovering from a cyberattack or security breach.

D

- **Data Encryption:** The process of converting information into a secure format that cannot be easily understood by unauthorised individuals.

- **Data Loss Prevention (DLP):** Strategies and tools used to ensure that sensitive data is not lost, misused, or accessed by unauthorised users, often involving monitoring and controlling data transfer.
- **Denial of Service (DoS) Attack:** An attack intended to shut down a machine or network, making it inaccessible to its intended users.
- **Distributed Denial of Service (DDoS) Attack:** A cyberattack where multiple systems flood the bandwidth or resources of a targeted system, usually one or more web servers, to overload it and make it unavailable to legitimate users.

E

- **Encryption Key Management:** The process of managing cryptographic keys in a cryptosystem, including their generation, exchange, storage, use, and replacement.
- **Endpoint Detection and Response (EDR):** Tools and solutions that monitor and collect data from endpoints (devices) to detect, investigate, and respond to potential security incidents.
- **Exfiltration:** The unauthorised transfer of data from a computer or network, often conducted by cybercriminals after gaining access to sensitive information.

F

- **Federated Identity Management (FIM):** A system that allows users to access multiple applications or systems using a single set of credentials, often across different domains or organisations.
- **Firewall:** A network security device that monitors and controls incoming and outgoing network traffic based on predetermined security rules.
- **Forensic Analysis:** The process of collecting, preserving, and analysing data from a computer system to investigate and recover information about security incidents or crimes.

G

- **Gap Analysis:** A method of assessing the differences between current performance and desired goals, particularly in the context of cybersecurity practices and compliance.
- **Governance, Risk, and Compliance (GRC):** A framework for managing an organisation's overall governance, enterprise risk management, and compliance with regulations.

H

- **Hashing:** A process that converts an input (or 'message') into a fixed-length string of characters, which is typically a hash code. Hashing is used to ensure data integrity.
- **Honeypot:** A security mechanism that creates a decoy system to attract and detect attackers, often used to study attack methods and improve defences.

I

- **Identity and Access Management (IAM):** A framework of policies and technologies for ensuring that the right individuals have appropriate access to technology resources.
- **Incident Response Plan (IRP):** A predefined, documented plan for responding to and managing security incidents to minimise impact and recover quickly.
- **Intrusion Detection System (IDS):** A device or software application that monitors a network or systems for malicious activity or policy violations.

J

- **Job Rotation:** A security practice where employees periodically rotate through different roles or responsibilities to prevent any one person from having unchecked power or knowledge of sensitive systems, reducing the risk of insider threats.

K

- **Key Performance Indicators (KPIs):** Quantifiable metrics used to evaluate the success of an organisation's cybersecurity strategies and initiatives.
- **Kill Chain:** A model originally used by the military to describe the structure of an attack. In cybersecurity, it refers to the steps of an attack, from initial reconnaissance to the final impact.

L

- **Layered Security (Defence in Depth):** A security strategy that employs multiple layers of defence to protect information and assets, ensuring that if one layer is compromised, others can provide necessary protection.
- **Least Privilege:** A principle in cybersecurity that states users should only have the minimum levels of access – or permissions – necessary to perform their job functions.

M

- **Malware:** Malicious software designed to disrupt, damage, or gain unauthorised access to a computer system, including viruses, worms, and Trojan horses.
- **Mitigation Strategy:** A plan or set of actions designed to reduce the severity, seriousness, or impact of something, particularly in the context of cyber threats.
- **Multi-Factor Authentication (MFA):** A security system that requires more than one method of authentication from independent categories of credentials to verify the user's identity for a login or other transaction.

N

- **Network Access Control (NAC):** A security solution that enforces policies on devices that access networks to improve security, typically by checking the device's security posture before allowing network access.

- **Network Segmentation:** The practice of dividing a computer network into smaller parts, or segments, to improve security and performance by limiting access and controlling traffic.

O

- **Open-Source Intelligence (OSINT):** Information collected from publicly available sources, often used in the context of gathering threat intelligence or conducting reconnaissance.
- **Operational Technology (OT):** Hardware and software that detects or causes changes through direct monitoring and control of physical devices, processes, and events in industrial environments.

P

- **Patch Management:** The process of managing a network of computers by regularly performing patch deployment to ensure security updates are applied to software to fix vulnerabilities.
- **Penetration Testing (Pen Testing):** A method of evaluating the security of a system by simulating an attack from a malicious source to identify vulnerabilities.
- **Phishing:** A type of social engineering attack where attackers pose as legitimate institutions to trick individuals into providing sensitive data such as usernames, passwords, or credit card numbers.

Q

- **Quarantine:** The process of isolating files or systems that are suspected to be infected or compromised, preventing the spread of malicious software or actions.

R

- **Ransomware:** A type of malware that encrypts the victim's data and demands payment (ransom) to restore access to the data or system.
- **Red Teaming:** A strategy where an organisation simulates a real-world attack scenario to test its defences and improve its security posture.
- **Risk Assessment:** The process of identifying, evaluating, and prioritising risks to an organisation's information systems and data to determine the appropriate level of security measures.

S

- **Secure Software Development Lifecycle (SSDLC):** A process that integrates security into every phase of software development, from planning and design to implementation, testing, and maintenance.
- **Security Awareness Training:** Programmes designed to educate employees about the risks associated with their actions in the digital environment and how to avoid actions that may compromise security.
- **Security Information and Event Management (SIEM):** A solution that provides real-time analysis of security alerts generated by applications and network hardware.
- **Security Token:** A physical device or software used in multifactor authentication to provide an additional layer of security by generating a unique code that must be entered along with the user's password.
- **SOC (Security Operations Centre):** A centralised unit that deals with security issues on an organisational and technical level by monitoring, detecting, analysing, and responding to cybersecurity incidents.
- **Supply Chain Attack:** A cyberattack that seeks to damage an organisation by targeting less secure elements in the supply chain, such as software updates or third-party vendors.

T

- **Third-Party Risk Management (TPRM):** The process of identifying, assessing, and controlling risks associated with outsourcing to third-party vendors or service providers.
- **Threat Intelligence:** The knowledge and data used to understand the threats that have, will, or are currently targeting the organisation, helping to inform decisions and enhance security measures.
- **Threat Modelling:** A process by which potential threats can be identified, enumerated, and prioritised, all as part of a structured approach to designing secure systems.
- **Two-Factor Authentication (2FA):** A type of multi-factor authentication that requires two distinct forms of identification before granting access.

U

- **Unified Threat Management (UTM):** An approach to information security where a single hardware or software installation provides multiple security functions, such as firewall, antivirus, and intrusion detection/prevention systems (IDPS).
- **User Behaviour Analytics (UBA):** The tracking, collecting, and assessing of user data and activities using monitoring systems to detect potential insider threats.

V

- **Virtual Private Network (VPN):** A secure network connection that allows users to connect to a network over the internet as if they were directly connected to the private network.
- **Vulnerability:** A weakness in a system, network, or application that can be exploited by threats to gain unauthorised access or cause harm.

W

- **Web Application Firewall (WAF):** A security device or service that filters and monitors HTTP traffic between a web application and the Internet, protecting web applications from attacks such as cross-site scripting (XSS) and SQL injection.
- **Whitelisting:** A security practice that allows only approved programs, IP addresses, or email addresses to be executed or access a system.

X

- **XML External Entity (XXE) Attack:** An attack targeting XML parsers that allows an attacker to exploit vulnerabilities in how XML data is processed, potentially leading to data exposure or system compromise.

Y

- **YubiKey:** A hardware authentication device that supports one-time passwords, public-key cryptography, and authentication, commonly used for two-factor authentication.

Z

- **Zero-Day Vulnerability:** A software vulnerability that is unknown to the vendor and has not been patched, which can be exploited by attackers until it is identified and fixed.
- **Zero Trust Architecture:** A security model that assumes no user, device, or system is trusted by default, requiring continuous verification of all entities attempting to access resources.

Appendix B

Additional Resources and References

This section provides a curated list of resources for further reading, professional development, to help you stay updated on the latest trends and best practices in cybersecurity.

Books and Publications

- *Cybersecurity and Cyberwar: What Everyone Needs to Know* by P.W. Singer and Allan Friedman
- *The Art of Deception: Controlling the Human Element of Security* by Kevin D. Mitnick
- *Information Security Management Principles* by Andy Taylor, David Alexander, Amanda Finch, and David Sutton

Websites and Online Courses

- *Cybrary*: Offers a wide range of cybersecurity courses and certifications.
- *Coursera*: Provides courses on cybersecurity fundamentals and advanced topics from leading universities.

- *Khan Academy*: Offers introductory courses on encryption and information security.

Industry Groups and Associations

- *Information Systems Audit and Control Association (ISACA)*: A global association that provides education and certification in information security.
- *International Information System Security Certification Consortium (ISC)*: Provides certifications like CISSP and offers a range of educational resources.
- *Open Web Application Security Project (OWASP)*: A nonprofit foundation that works to improve the security of software.

Government and Regulatory Bodies

- *National Institute of Standards and Technology (NIST)*: Develops standards and guidelines for cybersecurity practices.
- *European Union Agency for Cybersecurity (ENISA)*: Provides advice and recommendations on good cybersecurity practices in Europe.
- *Cybersecurity and Infrastructure Security Agency (CISA)*: The US agency responsible for protecting the nation's critical infrastructure from cyber threats.

Index